Pre-Schoolers with Autism

An Education and Skills Training Programme for Parents

of related interest

Relationship Development Intervention with Young Children
Social and Emotional Development Activities for Asperger Syndrome, Autism, PDD and NLD
Steven E. Gutstein and Rachelle K. Sheely
ISBN 1 84310 714 7

Small Steps Forward
Using Games and Activities to Help Your Pre-School Child with Special Needs
Sarah Newman
ISBN 1 85302 643 3
Winner: British Medical Association Popular Medical Book of the Year 2002

Assessing and Developing Communication and Thinking Skills in People with Autism and Communication Difficulties
A Toolkit for Parents and Professionals
Kate Silver, with Autism Initiatives
ISBN 1 84310 352 4

Making it a Success
Practical Strategies and Worksheets for Teaching Students with Autism Spectrum Disorder
Sue Larkey
Foreword by Tony Attwood
ISBN 1 84310 204 8

Playing, Laughing and Learning with Children on the Autism Spectrum
A Practical Resource of Play Ideas for Parents and Carers
Julia Moor
ISBN 1 84310 060 6

Giggle Time – Establishing the Social Connection
A Program to Develop the Communication Skills of Children with Autism, Asperger Syndrome and PDD
Susan Aud Sonders
Foreword by Andrew Gunsberg
ISBN 1 84310 716 3

Asperger's Syndrome in Young Children
A Developmental Guide for Parents and Professionals
Laurie Leventhal-Belfer and Cassandra Coe
ISBN 1 84310 748 1

Asperger's Syndrome
A Guide for Parents and Professionals
Tony Attwood
Foreword by Lorna Wing
ISBN 1 85302 577 1

Pre-Schoolers with Autism

An Education and Skills Training Programme for Parents

Manual for Parents

Avril V. Brereton and Bruce J. Tonge

Jessica Kingsley Publishers
London and Philadelphia

First published in 2005
by Jessica Kingsley Publishers
116 Pentonville Road
London N1 9JB, UK
and
400 Market Street, Suite 400
Philadelphia, PA 19106, USA

www.jkp.com

Copyright © Avril V. Brereton and Bruce J. Tonge 2005

Library of Congress Cataloging in Publication Data
Brereton, Avril V. (Avril Vaux), 1954-
    Pre-schoolers with autism : an education and skills training programme for parents : manual for parents / Avril V. Brereton and Bruce J. Tonge.
        p. cm.
    Includes bibliographical references and index.
    ISBN-10: 1-84310-342-7 (pbk.)
    ISBN-13: 978-1-84310-342-4 (pbk.)
    1. Autism in children. 2. Autistic children—Education (Early childhood) 3. Parents of autistic children. I. Tonge, Bruce J. (Bruce John) II. Title.
    RJ506.A9B74 2005
    649'.154—dc22
                                                                                        2004029525

British Library Cataloguing in Publication Data
A CIP catalogue record for this book is available from the British Library

ISBN-13: 978 1 84310 342 4
ISBN-10: 1 84310 342 7

Printed and Bound in Great Britain by
Athenaeum Press, Gateshead, Tyne and Wear

Contents

Acknowledgements

The development of *Pre-Schoolers with Autism: An Education and Skills Training Programme for Parents*, an evidence based intervention, was funded by the National Health and Medical Research Council of Australia (NH and MRC), Project Grant Number 124303.

Our thanks first go to the many families throughout Victoria and New South Wales who participated in the research project that developed and evaluated the programme. These families supported the programme at the stressful time shortly after their child had been given a diagnosis of autism. Their enthusiasm and commitment to our task was wonderful. We also thank the specialist autism assessment services in Melbourne (Monash Autism Assessment Programme), Geelong (at Gateways) and the North East Child and Adolescent Mental Health Service (NECAMHS).

Our thanks also go to the project staff who assessed children and families, ran parent intervention groups, managed the data base, analysed data and helped get the job done. Special thanks to Peter Enticott, Linda Brand, Jo-Ellen White, Dr Nicole Rinehart, Melissa Kiomall and Kerry Bull.

Introduction

This is a short 20-week course for parents who have a pre-schooler with autism. There are ten group sessions (usually about five families together) and, on alternate weeks, ten individual sessions.

Why do this course?

- To meet with other parents whose children have autism to share feelings and experiences.

- To learn more about autism.

- To learn how autism affects your child's daily life, communication, play and behaviour.

- To learn ideas for managing difficult behaviour.

- To learn how to communicate better with your child.

- To learn how to teach new social and play skills.

Parents' feedback:

'I liked meeting other people who were going through the same things as us and the programme helped us to understand our son better which made life easier and more enjoyable for the whole family.'

'Informative, well paced. I was able to discuss issues and swap strategies with other parents. There were lots of practical ideas and it was not full of theoretical information.'

'The fact that everyone had similar problems was a relief. It was a chance for me to get everything off my chest and ask questions. It also helped me to understand my son a lot better and subsequently I am a lot more patient and tolerant of his behaviour.'

Group Session 1

Outline and goals of the programme

→ Programme outline → Goals → Group rules → Discussion topic: Autism

Programme outline

This programme takes approximately five months to complete and involves families in weekly sessions for 20 weeks: ten small group sessions lasting 90 minutes and, on alternate weeks, ten sessions lasting one hour are held separately with each family. Session topics are listed below.

Group sessions (ten sessions)

Session 1 **Outline and goals of the programme**
Programme outline
Goals
Group rules
Discussion topic: Autism

Session 2 **Issues for parents after the diagnosis**
Reactions to diagnosis
Stress and coping

Session 3 **Understanding and managing difficult behaviour**
What is behaviour management?
How to start

Session 4 **How to change inappropriate behaviour by manipulating consequences**
Reinforcing behaviour
Extinction
Punishment

Session 5 **How to encourage new behaviour**
Prompting
Shaping
Chaining

Session 6 Communication problems in autism in verbal children
Verbal children
How do these language problems affect the behaviour of verbal children?

Session 7 Communication problems in autism in non-verbal children
Non-verbal children
How do these language problems affect the behaviour of non-verbal children?
Improving non-verbal communication using augmentative systems
How to encourage communication
Let's start communicating: Some ideas to get communication interaction going in young children

Session 8 Social impairment in autism
Treatment
Treatment approaches for young children
Treatment approaches for older children and adolescents

Session 9 How to work and play together
The importance of play
How to gain your child's attention
To increase eye contact, attending and staying on task, remember...

Session 10 Review and critique of programme – where next?

Individual sessions (ten sessions)

Session 1 An educational session with a focus on your child's development and behavioural symptoms

Session 2 Issues for parents after the diagnosis

Session 3 Understanding and managing difficult behaviour

Session 4 How to change inappropriate behaviour by manipulating consequences

Session 5 How to encourage new behaviour

Session 6 Communication problems in autism in verbal children

Session 7 Communication problems in autism in non-verbal children

Session 8 Social impairment in autism

Session 9 How to work and play together

Session 10 Review and critique of programme – where next?

The sessions cover a wide range of topics. Each topic is covered in a 'pair' of sessions (one group and one individual family).

Each group session is followed by an individual family session that allows you to explore the topic in relation to yourselves, your child and family.

The first two sessions introduce the programme and focus on teaching you more about autism and, in the individual sessions, provide an opportunity to discuss how autism affects your child in particular.

The following sessions explore important issues for parents such as parents' reaction to their child's diagnosis of autism, coping and managing grief and stress.

Sessions 3 to 5 focus on how to manage difficult behaviour and teach new skills. Group sessions will introduce new aspects of behaviour management and skills training each week and individual sessions will explore these further in direct relation to each child and family.

Sessions 6 to 9 focus on communication, social and attention problems associated with autism and what to do about them. Again, the individual sessions will relate what has been discussed in the group session to your child's particular needs.

Session 10 reviews the programme and provides parents with the opportunity to evaluate the programme and give feedback to the clinicians.

Goals

To give parents the opportunity to:

- learn more about autism and how it affects children

- talk about autism and how it affects the child and their family

- learn more about understanding and managing the child's emotional and behavioural problems

- learn how to teach the child new skills

- learn more about communicating well with the child

- learn more about community services and resources available for children with autism and their families.

Group rules

1. Participants must be punctual.
2. All discussion during the session is strictly confidential.
3. All participants have the right to speak.
4. Speakers will not be interrupted by other group members.
5. The session will end at the appointed time.

Discussion topic: Autism

What is autism?

Autism is a syndrome consisting of a set of developmental and behavioural features that must be present for the condition to be diagnosed.

The core features of autism include impairment in three main areas of functioning:

1. social interaction
2. communication
3. play and behaviour (restricted, repetitive and stereotyped patterns of behaviour, interests and activities).

(American Psychiatric Association 1994)

Kanner first described these core features in his paper of 1943 in which 11 children with 'autistic disturbances of affective contact' showed a distinctive pattern of symptoms:

1. inability to relate to people and situations
2. failure to use language for the purpose of communication
3. obsessive desire for the maintenance of sameness in the environment.

(Kanner 1943)

The DSM-IV (American Psychiatric Association 1994) diagnostic system emphasizes that symptoms may change throughout life and behaviour problems can range from severe to mild impairments.

What causes autism?

The cause of autism is unknown. It is a biological condition probably due to a number of causes acting together rather than one specific cause. It becomes obvious within the first 30 months of life. Autism affects the person throughout life.

SOME HISTORY

In the 1950s and early 1960s some (e.g. Bettelheim 1967) argued that autism was a schizophrenic withdrawal from reality and advocated residential centres for children, removing them from their families. Cold and rejecting parents were said to be causing autistic behaviour in their children and residential programmes were seen as a means of undoing autistic behaviours and establishing appropriate behaviours in their place. The treatment involved individual psychotherapy with the autistic child and attempts were made to change the parents and make them acknowledge their role in the development of the child's condition. Bettelheim (1967) referred to such a child as the 'empty fortress'. This 'psychogenic' theory and its treatment approaches fell from favour because it was not supported by evidence from systematic studies.

In the 1970s, new research highlighted basic cognitive deficits and organic brain dysfunction. This became known as the 'nature' theory of causation of autism and the bulk of the evidence pointed to a neurological (brain) dysfunction in autistic children.

Support for genetic influences on autism came from the research by Folstein and Rutter (1977), who undertook a study of 21 pairs of same-sex twins, one or both of whom had autism. The specific mode of inheritance is still unknown, but subsequent studies point to the likelihood that a number of genes are involved in creating the biological basis for autism.

WHAT WE NOW KNOW ABOUT CAUSES OF AUTISM

Research over the past 40 years has clarified a number of issues about the causes of autism. The psychogenic causation theory of the 1950s has been found to be lacking in evidence and dismissed. Evidence has made it clear that autism is a neurodevelopmental disorder involving basic cognitive and information processing deficits, affect, communication and social skills. Many questions remain unanswered regarding the neuropathophysiology of autism and the mode of genetic inheritance.

ASSOCIATED MEDICAL CONDITIONS

There is a frequent association between autism and a number of medical conditions that affect the brain, such as:

- pre- and perinatal trauma, neonatal asphyxia
- certain acquired encephalopathies and brain malformations
- metabolic disorders such as histidinemia, and Lesch-Nyhan syndrome
- genetic conditions and chromosomal abnormalities including Fragile X, tuberous sclerosis, Cornelia de Lange syndrome, Joubert syndrome, Williams syndrome and Hypomalanosis of Ito
- epilepsy.

Most importantly, there is an approximately 30 per cent risk of developing seizures (epilepsy) through childhood to early adulthood. The majority of persons with autism have non-specific abnormal electrical brain activity shown on an electro-encephalogram (EEG).

Some other medical conditions that lead to intellectual disability are rarely associated with autism, noticeably Down syndrome and cerebral palsy. The nature and meaning of the association between autism and these various other neurobiological conditions has yet to be determined.

Diagnosis of autism

Because the cause of autism is unknown, diagnosis relies upon matching the child's behaviour patterns and development with the diagnostic criteria. Autism usually emerges in early infancy, and the diagnosis of autism can be reliably made from two years of age. In 1980, the American Psychiatric Association's *Diagnostic and Statistical Manual* (DSM-III) introduced the diagnostic term pervasive developmental disorder (PDD) to cover a group of disorders of development including autism which presented with abnormalities and impaired functioning across the social, cognitive, emotional and language domains. These impairments were present from the first few years of life.

The DSM-IV (American Psychiatric Association 1994) includes five categories of pervasive developmental disorders (PDDs):

- Autistic disorder (autism)
- Asperger's disorder
- Rett's disorder
- Childhood disintegrative disorder
- Pervasive developmental disorder – not otherwise specified (PDD-NOS).

See Appendix 2 for a brief description of these.

How common is autism?

Prevalence estimates for autism have been gathered for over 30 years. At least 23 prevalence studies have been reported in the literature from 1966 to 1997. These studies use varying diagnostic criteria as definitions of autism have changed over time and population samples have varied in size and type.

The autism rate for studies published between 1966 and 1991 was 4.4 per 10,000. Recent works with the most rigorous ascertainment methods have consistently yielded rates of about 10 per 10,000 (Fombonne 2003). It has been suggested that the prevalence of autism is increasing; however, improved community awareness and assessment, together with changes in diagnostic practice, may have increased the number identified. Study design and methodology may also contribute to increased prevalence rates in some cases. The prevalence rate for unspecified PDDs and PDD-NOS is 15 per 10,000. Fombonne's (2003) estimate for all 'autism spectrum disorders' is 27.5 per 10,000.

Reports of autism 'outbreaks' raise the question as to whether autism might be the result of some environmental risk or other factors. There have been reports of links between the onset of autism and the administration of the MMR (measles, mumps, rubella) vaccination. Several recent studies have found no association. The link between MMR and autism has not been confirmed by any robust study to date. Tidmarsh and Volkmar (2003) recently discussed the controversy regarding high levels of mercury in children with autism and the use of thimerosol in vaccines. The hypothesis is that the neurotoxic effects of mercury produce neurodevelopmental problems in vulnerable children. There is no evidence that children exposed to mercury from any source have a higher rate of autism. Furthermore, thimerosol was removed from vaccines in the US, Japan and Canada in the early 1990s yet prevalence rates of autism have been reported to have risen since that time.

What about social class, race or gender?

Fombonne (2003) reports that recent epidemiological studies have failed to support Kanner's early theory that social class and level of parental education were associated with autism. Rates of autism are similar throughout the world with no higher prevalence reported in any particular racial group. Autism is approximately four times more common in boys than girls. Despite this striking male predominance, there has been no research evidence to account for this sex ratio but it might point to an X chromosome link.

Assessment

It is clear from the DSM-IV diagnostic criteria that the diagnosis requires a comprehensive, multidisciplinary assessment comprising at least:

- developmental and family history
- observation of the child's behaviour and interaction with others
- a medical assessment including tests for known causes of developmental delay (e.g. chromosome analysis) and hearing tests
- a cognitive assessment using appropriate tests such as Psychoeducational Profile–Revised (PEP-R) (Schopler *et al.* 1990) and Wechsler Pre-school and Primary Scale of Intelligence–Revised (WPPSI-R) (Wechsler 1989)
- a structured language assessment
- the use of structured assessment tools such as the Autism Diagnostic Instrument (ADI) and Observational Scales (ADOS) (Le Couteur *et al.* 1989; Lord *et al.* 1989), clinician completed rating scales such as the Childhood Autism Rating Scale (CARS) (Schopler *et al.* 1980), and parent or teacher completed checklists such as the Developmental Behaviour Checklist (DBC) (Einfeld and Tonge 1992)
- comprehensive and sensitive feedback to the parents and carers about the diagnosis as the first step in developing a plan of intervention and service provision.

See *Diagnostic and Statistical Manual of Mental Disorders*, 4th Edition, 1994, Washington DC: American Psychiatric Association, pp. 70–71, for the specific diagnostic criteria.

Individual Session 1

An educational session with a focus on your child's development and behavioural symptoms

Tasks for this session

- Are there any queries you have about your child's assessment and diagnosis?

- Read through the assessment reports you have. Are there any parts you wish to discuss further?

- In this session we will be focusing our discussion on your child's profile of autism symptoms.

Group Session 2

Issues for parents after the diagnosis

→ Reactions to diagnosis   → Stress and coping

Reactions to diagnosis

Reactions to the diagnosis of autism vary from family to family just as the road that leads each family to diagnosis can be different. In some cases the parents are aware that their child is slow in achieving developmental milestones, for example at three years of age their child may have no speech, and instigate the assessment and diagnosis process themselves. For others, concerns may be raised by a relative who knows the child well or a professional such as a pre-school teacher who expresses concerns about the child's play or social skills and suggests some further assessment.

For some parents the wait has been long (up to two years from the time they first had an idea that something may be wrong with their child) and for them a sense of relief comes with the diagnosis when they finally find out what the problem is, that it has a name and that the process of accessing appropriate services and support can begin. Some parents have read widely and already have a strong suspicion that their child has autism by the time the formal diagnosis is made. In these families, some intervention plans may already be in place and the parents are well on the way to adjusting to their child's difficulties.

The diagnosis may come as a shock to some parents who did not seek an assessment but were referred by a health professional or teacher. They may not believe it, be angry with the professionals who have made the diagnosis and reject it totally. Some parents may be overwhelmed by feelings of sadness and guilt. Some families we have worked with are initially more concerned about the reaction from members of the extended family and worry about how to tell them rather than thinking of their own feelings at this time.

What *is* common to all families is the need for accurate information about autism and the services which are available to them. Families can be extremely vulnerable to those who offer 'cures' at this time. Information about early intervention services for the child, local parent support groups, access to parent training and education, education for carers and other professionals involved with the child, family support and respite care are all important.

Stress and coping

Autism is associated with considerable personal suffering and is a significant burden and stress for parents, families and carers. Stress and anxiety have been found to be higher in parents of children with autism when compared to parents of children with other intellectual and developmental disabilities and can adversely impact upon family functioning and mental health, including stress on marital relationships. Several studies have found that mothers of children with autism were at a significantly greater risk of developing clinical depression than mothers of children with intellectual disability (ID) without autism and typically developing children.

Clearly, we need to find ways to help parents and carers of children with autism. Harris (1994) suggested some buffers to help families and carers adapt to the special needs of the child with autism:

- effective coping skills (parent training)

- a good social support network

- family cohesion.

Effective coping skills (parent training)

Young pre-school aged children spend most of their time with their family at home. Children with autism are no different from other young children in this respect. It therefore makes good sense to help parents and carers improve their day-to-day coping skills. Centre-based early intervention (EI) programmes are certainly important but, considering the majority of the child's time will be spent with parents/carers at home and not at the local EI centre, we need to help families manage daily life with their children in the home setting.

One coping strategy that has been shown to be effective for parents of children with autism is parent training to teach families the kinds of management procedures that will enable them to understand and control their child's disruptive behaviours and increase the parents' abilities to help their child master new adaptive, play communication and social skills. Research on the effects of structured and systematic parent training, such as the 'Pre-Schoolers with Autism' programme, has shown that parents can learn these skills and become more effective teachers for their children (Koegel, Bimbela and Schreibman 1996; Moes and Frea 2002). Importantly, this type of programme is also effective in lowering parental stress and improving parental mental health. Parents report that knowing 'what to do and how to do it' makes them feel more in control and positive in their parenting skills.

A good social support network

Some families have found that a support group that enables members to share their feelings and emotional responses, and enlarge their social networks to include other families who can help when things are tough, is very helpful. Support groups can also be a focus for ongoing educational programmes and social activities for the family. A support group that helps parents to learn how to utilize community resources and advocate on behalf of themselves is also important.

Sibling support groups can be helpful in exploring the issues confronted by brothers and sisters of the child with autism. Not all sibling responses are negative. For example, teaching siblings the skills to enable them to play with their brother or sister can be beneficial for the whole family. Some siblings report that caring for a brother or sister with autism has helped increase their self esteem, sense of empathy and interpersonal skills. Siblings should not be expected to take over parenting roles or responsibilities but the sibling support group can provide the opportunity for older siblings to learn some basic management skills. Issues such as understanding what autism is and why the child with autism behaves as he/she does, feelings of jealousy because of the attention that the child with autism receives, anger about rejection by their peers and worry about the 'inheritance' of autism can be discussed in a sibling support group.

Family cohesion

Parents can have different reactions to having a child with autism. Research has shown that mothers experience a greater personal impact than fathers who have a child with autism. Most often the mother has the responsibility of child rearing and the father has work outside the home. This may account for the difference between mothers' and fathers' perceptions of the impact on their lives of having a child with autism. A recent study found that fathers were more upset by the stress their wives experienced than by being the father of a child with autism.

It has been found that the mother's life satisfaction is enhanced when the father assumes his fair share of care of the child. Feeling emotionally supported by one's partner is important when trying to respond to and meet the special needs of the child with autism. Adjusting to these needs can bring additional stress to all the members of the family.

Each family member, siblings as well as parents, need their own space and parents need time together. Making the time available for this space can be difficult and the challenge is to find a balance between closeness and distance, between being part of the family and being a separate person. Planned, regular respite care as well as enlisting the support of a social network can be helpful in achieving this.

Here are some personal accounts from parents of young children with autism. The first is a father's reaction to his son's diagnosis and the second is a mother's account of life with two young children with autism (reproduced with permission).

Jez – My feelings about Jez from the day he was diagnosed 'autistic' (written by Garry)

The first day I was very emotional. I couldn't even start the car to go to work. I stayed home that day.

I then thought I had gotten over that initial feeling but have found it coming back to me especially when I see a movie, TV shows or even hear or read stories about autistic adults. For some stupid reason I place Jez in their shoes and think that is how he could end up and that's when the odd tear builds up in my eye. But partial denial, the old 'he'll be OK, he'll fight this and nobody will even know he's autistic', creeps back into my mind. But unfortunately there will always be that doubt. I know if I talked about my feelings with anyone I would be a blubbering mess. Being a six-foot man, I don't think you are meant to do this.

I find him both frustrating and amazing. Frustrating for both him and me, when he's trying to tell me something, and not being able to understand what it is he is saying. It is frustrating for me because I can hear the frustration in his voice. But I find him amazing in what he can draw and remember, like the alphabet and counting to 20, spelling certain words, and streetscapes he continually draws. It is these amazing things that make me feel good inside and these are the things I tell people at work he can do.

With the news a couple of weeks ago about him being in the 20 per cent group of autistic children that are intellectually normal and has the capacity of learning was a great weight off my mind. But then I have this stupid feeling, is he an exceptional copier and all the things he did on the assessment day, did he do it with his own intellect or was it routine? But I know it was his intellect.

Like I've stated before there is always something there in the back of my mind. With anxiety I'll always have that burning question. Who'll look after him when I'm gone? But I know he'll be OK (I hope).

It's been hard writing this (emotion wise) but I've surprised myself and done it. But this is how I feel from the first day until now. How I feel later, who knows? We'll just have to see how Jez grows up.

The adventures of 'Connor McGoo' (and family) (written by Kim)

Hi there. I came into this world with my hands clasped under my chin and one tiny squawk. My first nick-name was 'little professor' because I was quiet, wrinkled and had large, wise brown eyes. Well that was the first day of my life anyway. From that day forward, however, I have been known by a number of different aliases and have tried my hand at many different careers (some with STUNNING results).

My first career began when I was two days old. I was sent forward as a secret agent to further test just how much sleep deprivation and cardiac stimulation my parents could sustain. I was also involved in attempting to break the sound barrier with the human voice. I was very successful in this field, managing to sleep for only 15 to 20 minute intervals followed by hours of relentless screaming (oh, and occasionally turning my whole body blue which gave my parents a good heart stress test). My co-agent (my elder sister) had been successfully carrying out the afore-mentioned mission for the previous three and a half years but hey, I couldn't let her have all the fun.

Mum and Dad had been taking her to doctors since she was a small baby but they rarely got listened to because they were just ignorant and inexperienced first parents, right. I mean, these doctors had medical degrees and Mum and Dad only lived with us basically 24 hours a day. So, our cover was safe for now. At least it was until we reached Wodonga but that's another story.

My next career was to test how well every man-made product stood up to the test of being bashed repeatedly against other objects and I was appropriately re-nicknamed 'bam-bam'. It was easy to also keep assuming my secret agent cover on the sleep deprivation front as well.

Interior decorating was the next phase of my amazing careers. I tried out many innovative concepts including repainting feature walls in jam, honey and especially weet-bix which was the only food I would eat for breakfast, lunch and dinner. Yep, those were the days. Nothing like wearing a kilo tub of honey all over your body then transferring it 'creatively' to other internal surfaces.

It was also pretty good seeing the frustration of the 'experienced' child nurses who said they'd get me to eat new things. After almost three days without eating anything (except for a pseudo-toddler milk formula) my victory was soooooo sweet. Oh and the cornflakes and crushed eggs on the floor created just that little something extra (but my older sister takes credit for that innovation).

Soon after, I discovered that I was probably going to be the next 'Pro Hart' (an Australian painter). This realisation hit me after I up-ended a large tin of fire-engine red powdered paint, followed by a tin of canary yellow paint onto the two-year-old champagne beige carpet in my sister's room. Mum was speechless (well, for a full five seconds anyway).

I was also quite successful at seeing just how much force can be exerted on five-point leather harnesses until they snap. Hint: make sure that the surface on which your face is going to connect is not concrete. Results: stitches in chin without anaesthetic and a long-lasting fear of white surgical gloves.

Around that time I also developed my first political opinions. We lived in Townsville and I got to meet the Prime Minister of Australia and the leader of the opposition. I waited until Prime Minister Howard was face to face with me then I let out the biggest tongue-raspberry sound/spit and yell I could muster. One of the reporters nearby said to Mum 'it seems he's started his political aspirations early'. I believe it was at that point that Mum grew a long neck, spurred claws and feathers but the beach was 300 metres away and even an ostrich wouldn't try to stick their head into the pavement.

At the ripe old age of three I experimented with becoming a dancing instructor. Method: take one large furry black cat and add copious amounts of jumbled up sticky tape to the paws and fur in general. Then, stand back and watch an amazing version of 'shake your tail feather', the 'Mexican hat dance' and cha-cha all in one. Hint: be prepared to run like Patrick Johnstone when Mum hears the cat crying in distress.

Speaking of speed, I conducted (on four separate occasions) an experiment involving seeing how quickly drivers could stop a vehicle in order to avoid hitting me as I ran straight out in front of them. Hint: this also allows a good voice projection and heart acceleration test for parents.

Mum and Dad were always careful about sharp objects as I attempted to develop my skills as an opportunistic surgeon. One day, Mum was interrupted from her gardening and placed the secateurs up high whilst she chatted briefly with a client. Using my amazing speed I brought over the wheel barrow, the catcher from the mower and a box and seized the surgical instrument. Suddenly I let go my pre-operative throat scream and Mum (and the client) turned to find me with the secateurs firmly shut (through my t-shirt) and sticking out of my abdomen. Luckily my scrub-nurse (my mother) came running with a wadded up tea-towel and calmly released my operating tool. My skills paid off. There was just a tiny nick as I had mostly pinched the skin. Upon turning around, my mother had to go to the aid of the client who was close to fainting.

One of my recent attempts at a career change involved an experimental bungee jump off the massage table. Hint: make sure you jump down (not sideways) especially when there is a plate glass window and solid ledge in the way. Results: being rushed to hospital and having a mighty sore head for about a week.

These are some of my numerous adventures and they are sure to continue.

My mother only has two grey hairs (yes, she counted them) and both her and Dad have good blood pressure which I find amazing (so do they). The big 'kahuna' gave me a cheeky, loveable personality and large brown eyes which I guess is some consolation and makes it easy to love me despite my secret agent activities.

I am now five and a half and my older sister is nine. At present we are still attempting to train our younger sister to be a better secret agent. She has taken well to some of our methods but, somehow, there is a difference. My older sister and I have both been diagnosed with autism in the last twelve months and Mum and Dad were finally able to piece together why things had happened the way they had. The daily challenges finally made sense and they were welcomed into a community of people who gave their understanding, compassion and companionship.

Mum reckons there is no perfection in humanity except for our ability to love unconditionally and the daily striving to overcome our challenges. We are far more than simply a diagnosis. It is one tiny step in the millions of steps we take toward our true potential as human beings as we constantly grow, shape and change every day. Some of these changes may be so subtle that others may not even notice but they are there just the same. Every single experience and reaction in life defines us at each and every given moment of time.

Our parents have had many moments of heartache, anger and despair. However, these same moments of anguish make it possible to turn every small achievement into great ones – moments of pure elation. The anger gives us the momentum to move forward. The heartache, compassion for others and despair, the balancing depth to which we can truly appreciate the heights of happiness.

Living with daily challenges strips the soul bare and allows us the chance to truly take the time to see what is most precious and most important. They give us great power to learn from what is put before us and to find ways to change what we can. Our destinies are forever changing and our personal will and spirit have a great impact on what the final outcomes will be.

Here are some thoughts from a teenager about his younger brother.

Russ
(written by Brendan)

OK, let me describe to you a situation that occurs frequently in my household. I lie on my bed, talking trivial yet highly enjoyable dribble [sic] into the end of a telephone to my girlfriend. She is stressed, and I, being the sensitive, caring boyfriend I try to be, am trying to comfort her. She is at the peak of her emotional eruption when the door of my room bursts open, and my brother steps through. 'Brendan' he says in an urgent semi-whisper.

Frustration arises in me as I calmly ask my girlfriend to hold on and put my hand over the phone. 'What?' I hiss through clenched teeth, directing a fierce stare straight at him.

There's no way he can't tell I'm pissed off, and yet this does not seem to faze him. 'Eminem is coming to Melbourne. I just saw an ad on TV, and he's comin' on the 26th.'

I look at him blankly for a moment.

'That's all you came to tell me?'

'Yeah I just thought I'd…'

'Get out of my room.'

This does not seem to faze him either. As he closes the door, I see the look on his face, a big grin as he converts from the external world to the internal. His thoughts consume him. He probably has forgotten already that he ever interrupted me.

This is the world of my brother. It would be an interesting experience, I think, to be my brother. He is forever retreating into his little world, and I have come up with three reasons why. First, escape – especially during an argument with me, when you can see him retreat and start going through his mind what he should have said to me but didn't. Second, amusement – when he's bored, there is no stopping him. And there is the third reason, when he gets excited, it's virtually impossible to get his attention.

I've come to recognize the physical changes that take place as his internal thoughts take over. The ever-growing smile. The unfocused eyes. If he's re-enacting a scene in his head, he'll make puppets out of his hands and turn them into characters in a scene, holding them in front of his face, mouthing words and sentences. He sometimes does laps of a room, of even the whole house. It's as if another person is waiting to burst out of him.

His thoughts aren't weird or crazy. When he tells me his thoughts, they are imaginative, creative and, most often, highly amusing. He's a bright, happy kid.

Nothing is strange about the way he thinks. He is very naive about certain topics that he doesn't understand, which makes some of the things he talks about a bit weird. But other than that, he's fine. It's only that he's continuously shifting from the outer to the inner world. For a regular person, it is said that we daydream every ninety minutes or so. My brother, I have observed, can daydream, for short periods, several times every five minutes.

Russell's condition doesn't bother me. Hell, I've grown up with him. I'm so used to it that I look at the way other brothers and sisters communicate, and wonder what it would be like to communicate with someone on the same wavelength. Sure, we act like normal brothers do — forever arguing, fighting over ownership, complaining to Mum about something the other sibling has done. For example, a pet peeve of mine is when I wake up and look forward to the idea of toast for breakfast, only to find that Russ, who has a love of bread, has used up the last of it. This is a normal brotherly thing.

But when it comes to conversation, it's a different matter. I have to continually find simpler, easier, or just better ways to get Russell to understand something. Once he's got it, though, he's fine. He has an unbelievable memory. It's just a matter of storing the information in there in a way that makes sense.

But like I said, none of this bothers me. But I do worry about my brother. People who know him, who know how he is and what he's like, always complain when I try to stop Russell from doing the little things that he does, like talking to himself, which he can't really help. They seem to think that I don't accept the way he is, and am trying to stop him for that reason. But that's not it at all. It's just that, on more than one occasion, I have witnessed the stares, the laughs and the sideways glances that he gets because of those little things. And I don't like the way those people can't see that he is a normal kid. Well, that he is to me. I want them to look at him the way they would anyone else. Because he is just like everyone else.

He's my brother, and he has autism. It's only mild, luckily. People who have it bad are almost completely locked in their internal mind, and hardly communicate at all. So I'm glad he's only got a little bit of it.

He's my brother and he's a little different.

But I can't imagine life without him.

Individual Session 2
Issues for parents after the diagnosis

Tasks for this session

- In light of the discussion in the last group session and what you have read so far, are there any particular things you would like to talk about today?

- Make a list and bring it to the session.

Task 1: Things I would like to talk about from the last group session and what I have been reading

Group Session 3
Understanding and managing difficult behaviour

→ What is behaviour management?   → How to start

What is behaviour management?

- It is a technique for changing behaviour; that is, the things children do that we can see and describe.

- It tells you *how* to teach rather than *what* to teach.

- It is about teaching methods that suit the child.

- It shows if the strategy is working or not because we can measure change.

- Behaviour management is *careful teaching*.

But…

- It is not necessarily a cure-all. It requires commitment and a change in your approach.

- It is not prescriptive – there is not a set answer for a particular problem. Good observational skills need to be developed to help work out why the child is doing what he or she is doing.

Principles of behaviour theory

- Behaviour theory maintains that behaviour is learned according to what happens after the behaviour (the *consequence*).

- A positive consequence will tend to increase the chance of the behaviour happening again.

- A negative consequence will tend to reduce the chance of the behaviour happening again.

Behaviour management as a treatment for autism

Treatment based on the principles of learning has proven to be an effective means of teaching children with autism. This type of treatment of behavioural problems was first reported in the 1960s, when the emphasis was on eliminating problem behaviours. A combination of rewards and punishments was used. Schreibman (1994) described the behavioural approach to teaching children with autism in terms of autism being a syndrome comprised of specific behavioural excesses and deficits. For example, behavioural excesses are behaviours that are inappropriate or occur at an intensity or frequency that is inappropriate. A behavioural deficit is a behaviour that does not occur at adequate strength or those that are not exhibited and whose absence is inappropriate. For example, behavioural excesses in autism include self-stimulation, obsessions, and self-injurious behaviour. Examples of behavioural deficits in autism include language and social deficits and difficulties attending to task.

In traditional behaviour therapy, once the behavioural problem is studied, demonstrated and understood, the environment is manipulated in such a way as to increase, decrease or maintain the behaviour. What is known as the ABC approach follows. The **B**ehaviour to be managed or modified is described, and then the **A**ntecedents, or what happens *before* the behaviour occurs, and the **C**onsequences, or what happens *after* the behaviour, are manipulated. The child's treatment programme comprises a set of procedures designed to address the specific behavioural excesses and deficits exhibited by that child.

Understanding what the difficult behaviour is telling us

Those who work with children with autism and their families have found that the traditional approach to behaviour therapy is useful but not always easy to implement because it can be very difficult to work out the antecedent and consequence of the difficult behaviour.

For example, a child with autism may suddenly scream when out shopping. The screaming may be because on an earlier trip to the shops the child heard a loud noise at this particular place and now associates the place with something unpleasant from the past. No amount of observation will help in understanding the present behaviour.

Behaviour management programmes today take into account more than the ABC approach and look at individual variables, environmental factors and how the child's ability to communicate is affecting his/her behaviour. A current approach is to try to understand the *function* or *purpose* of the child's behaviour and what the child is trying to tell us; that is, the *communicative function* of the behaviour.

Difficult behaviour is sometimes referred to as *challenging behaviour*. Perhaps it is better to regard it as being a challenge for us to understand what the behaviour means. Aggression, self-injury, and stereotypic and other disruptive behaviours may have a number of communicative functions including:

- to indicate the need for help or attention

- to escape from stressful situations or activities

- to obtain desired objects

- to protest against unwanted events/activities

- to obtain stimulation.

If the function of the behaviour can be worked out, then it is possible to substitute the undesirable behaviour with a more desirable way to get his/her message across. We know that children with autism have severe social and communication deficits, together with a need for ritual and routine. This combination of difficulties leads to behavioural problems in most children with autism. Howlin (1998) discussed behavioural problems associated with autism in relation to the principal diagnostic features of autism and areas of deficit:

- impairment in communication and understanding

- impaired social understanding

- obsessions and ritualistic behaviours.

IMPAIRMENT IN COMMUNICATION AND UNDERSTANDING

If the child does not have adequate language to get his message across it is likely that he will become frustrated and this may lead to aggression in some children. In other children who have limited speech, the emergence of echolalia or verbal routines and obsessive questioning may result. Difficult behaviour can also be associated with problems in the child's understanding of language. Poor understanding can be associated with increased anxiety, distress and disruptive behaviour.

A misunderstanding: Jon aged four

Jon's mum reported:

> Jon loves to go to kindergarten. He has a special pair of shoes he wears to kindergarten. He has some speech but doesn't follow instructions very well. His mother cleaned his kindergarten shoes and put them by the front door and said: 'We'll be going to kinder this afternoon.'
>
> Jon began crying loudly about ten minutes later and his mother couldn't work out why. He couldn't tell her what was wrong when she asked and eventually he went to his room, got his kindergarten satchel and stood at the door.
>
> Jon's mum then realized that he had not understood what she had said as she put his shoes by the door. Jon saw the shoes and thought he must be going to kindergarten straight away. He didn't understand the 'this afternoon' part of the message and so became very upset. This was a reminder to Jon's mum that she has to be careful to make sure that Jon understands what she says by keeping sentences short and using pictures.

IMPAIRED SOCIAL UNDERSTANDING

Lack of social awareness can result in a child with autism being withdrawn and isolated from his peers. In others this lack of awareness may prompt disruptive or aggressive behaviour, for example, towards a child who may approach to play together or share an activity.

The non-party: Susan aged five

Susan's mum reported:

> Susan had a birthday party and ten children she knew from kindergarten were invited to her home. Mum had planned some simple party games and Susan's favourite video and food. When the children arrived, Susan went outside and would not join in any of the party activities and sat at the top of her slide.

OBSESSIONS AND RITUALISTIC BEHAVIOURS

Some children are so involved with their rituals and obsessions that there is no time in the day to learn play skills or other age appropriate behaviour. Some children, when routines are disrupted, become distressed and even aggressive towards the person who has interrupted the obsessive preoccupation or ritual while others do everything they can to restore the routine. Many children with autism also dislike change which may lead to very rigid and inflexible patterns of behaviour. When change occurs these children can become distressed and anxious.

The great line-up: Brendan aged six

Brendan's mum reported:

> Brendan loves to line things up, he doesn't play with his toys. He can spend an entire day lining up objects in the hallway that leads from the front door to the back door of the house. One day Brendan began a 'line' early in the morning. He busily fetched all sorts of household items, pieces of clothing, furniture and toys. The family cat, Hector, was asleep in the hallway and became part of the line. Brendan got the line to the back door and was satisfied that the job was done. *But*... Hector woke up and wanted to go outside. Well, Brendan was very unhappy about this and began to scream. He was very distressed and kept putting the cat back in line. The cat also became very upset and Mum had to intervene. The only solution was to find his sister's toy cat and place it there. Peace was restored. Brendan stopped screaming.

How to start

It can be difficult to know just where to start when you are considering trying to change your child's behaviour. It may seem as though the entire day is filled with a series of disastrous episodes. Confidence and success are very important for everyone at this stage, for you, your child with autism and the rest of the family who are experiencing the home situation.

Start with a behaviour that you think you have a pretty good chance of doing something about. It may in fact *not* be the behaviour that is causing the most trouble for both you and your child, but it is a way of easing all of you into the new world of behaviour management.

A successful outcome for everyone when you are starting out helps you feel more confident and ready to tackle other behaviours that may be more entrenched or difficult to assess in terms of their ABC pattern and purpose.

Choosing and setting goals

We know from many years of working with young children and their families that teaching children in a 'naturalistic setting', rather than in a formal setting such as sitting at a table, leads to a better chance of success in changing a behaviour and teaching new skills. The behaviour you want to work on will therefore be chosen and a plan developed so you can work on that behaviour as it occurs in a natural way throughout the day, rather than setting aside a particular time and restricting teaching to that time.

DEFINE THE BEHAVIOUR

Remember, behaviour is an action or series of actions performed by a person. These actions are both observable and describable.

DESCRIBE THE BEHAVIOUR OBJECTIVELY

Remember, a behaviour must be described in very specific words so that the behaviour could be identified, observed and measured in the same way by yourself or others.

Describe exactly what your child does. Describe only what you see (observe). Stay away from feelings, intuitions etc. Here are some examples:

Incorrect: 'He's having a tantrum.'

Correct: 'He's lying on his back on the floor screaming, kicking his legs and banging his hands together.'

Incorrect: 'I think she's being stubborn.'

Correct: 'When I ask her to sit down she shouts *no*.'

WORK OUT THE ABC PATTERN/FUNCTION OF THE BEHAVIOUR

You will need to describe carefully what happens *before* the behaviour occurs and what happens straight *after* the behaviour.

Write it down each time so you have a record. Also consider what your child is getting out of this behaviour. For example, is he/she getting your attention by doing this? Is he/she letting you know he/she is tired or hungry but does not have enough words to tell you? That is, does the behaviour seem to have a *function* that you have not noticed or thought about? It is also important to record how often the behaviour occurs to get some idea of the frequency of the behaviour.

Some statements from parents about daily life with their child

Do these sound familiar to you?

'He's no problem at all during the day. He just sits and watches his favourite videos over and over. He doesn't even seem to get hungry or thirsty so I take his morning tea and lunch over to him. Mind you, if we have to go out all hell breaks loose.'

'Everything seems to take so long and we battle over each little thing I ask her to do. Getting dressed is the worst. She will not co-operate at all and sometimes even pulls her clothes off just when I have finally got them on.'

'Sometimes I wonder if he was born to make my life hell.'

'When Paul started to talk things became a lot easier. Now I don't have to guess all the time.'

'We get so excited about little improvements because they are giant leaps for Katie. Now that she can sit in her chair and eat at the table with us we do something together as a whole family every night that other families probably never even think about.'

Working out the reason for the behaviour: James aged five

James' mum reported:

James had some children from pre-school at home for a play. They had been twice before and each time there was trouble because James kept dropping blocks on their heads (only very small Lego blocks, but it was annoying and the visitors didn't like it).

I tried several things. First I was cross with James and told him to stop dropping blocks on the children. He stopped and went away to play by himself on the computer so that was no good. I had invited the children so that they could play together and have a happy time. The next time it happened I gave the other children attention and hoped that this might stop James from dropping blocks on them. That didn't work either as all he did was cry.

I looked for the ABC pattern here. Obviously my consequences were not helping to change James' behaviour so perhaps it was the antecedent that needed looking at.

Next time the children came over I watched for what was happening. The children came to the play room and began to tip out all the blocks on the floor and make things with them. James watched this and stood beside the children watching them play. They ignored him. He didn't say anything to them and after watching them for about five minutes he started with the block dropping. It dawned on me…he wanted to play too but didn't know how to join in.

I called James over to where I was and said to him: 'If you want to play you have to say to the kids, "I want to play blocks too."' We practiced this and then he tried it. We went over and he said to the children: 'I want to play blocks too.' They moved over and made a space for him on the floor and they played happily side by side.

Sometimes it's easy to forget that kids with autism just don't know how to play with other kids so they end up doing the wrong thing. There I'd been working on the consequences and I should have been thinking about *why* James was dropping blocks. Learning your ABCs is important!

Individual Session 3

Understanding and managing difficult behaviour

What is daily life like with your child? Observe your child's behaviour and determine the ABC pattern. Why does it happen and what happens next?

Tasks for this session

- Do any of the parent statements in the session notes particularly reflect how *you* feel?

- Watch your child (behavioural observations) and make a list of behaviours describing each behaviour clearly and objectively. (Look back at the examples in Group Session 3 notes.)

- Add the ABC pattern to this list by watching for what happens *before* the behaviour and what happens *after*.

- Try to do this with at least two behaviours over a couple of days.

Task 1: Parent statements that reflect how I feel too

Task 2: Behaviours I have observed during the week

1.

2.

3.

4.

Task 3: ABC pattern of behaviours I have observed during the week

Antecedent (what happened before)	Behaviour	Consequence (what happened after)

Group Session 4

How to change inappropriate behaviour by manipulating consequences

→ Reinforcing behaviour   → Extinction   → Punishment

There are times when *all* children do things we would prefer them not to.

Before you embark on changing or replacing behaviours, careful consideration must be given to just how difficult the behaviour is for both the child and those who live and work with him/her.

Behaviour is inappropriate if it endangers the child or others and increases the likelihood of social rejection or isolation. It is also inappropriate if engaging in the particular behaviour interferes with or precludes the child from being able to participate in enjoyable activities and an educational programme.

Disruptive and self-injurious behaviours sometimes occur in children with autism. The sooner these can be replaced with new and acceptable behaviours, the better. We know that the longer children engage in inappropriate behaviours, the more difficult it can be to change them or replace them with more acceptable ones.

There are two ways of approaching how to change behaviour. We can either change the consequence (what happens *after* the behaviour) or the antecedent (what happens *before* the behaviour). The most common approach is to change or manipulate consequences. There are several ways to do this which we shall explore.

Today, there is an emphasis on increasing appropriate behaviours rather than removing inappropriate ones, so that each child can build up a repertoire of 'good' behaviour. As the good behaviours increase, the inappropriate ones are replaced and therefore decrease over time.

Reinforcing behaviour

Positive reinforcement is the easiest and most often used method of strengthening a desirable behaviour. By following the behaviour with a pleasant event we are increasing the likelihood of that behaviour occurring again. One of the trickiest things here is to work out what the child actually finds pleasant. We must not assume that what we find pleasant and rewarding will be shared by others, particularly children with autism. For example, we may find attention in the form of a hug and a kiss very pleasant, but for the child with autism this may actually be experienced as unpleasant and overwhelming.

Parents usually know what their children like and enjoy. It is a good idea to make a list of activities and things that your child finds pleasant that can be used as reinforcers.

Extinction

The most common approach to decreasing a behaviour is by *extinction*. This means that a behaviour which has previously been followed by a reinforcer or reward is no longer followed by this. For example, when the child has a tantrum and Dad gives in and gives him what he wants (the reinforcer) the tantrums will continue because they get the child what he wants. Using extinction, the parent no longer responds and gives the reinforcer.

Warning: when you begin using extinction to remove a behaviour, it usually gets worse before it gets better. This is because the child will try *even harder* to get the reinforcer that used to come. It takes a while for the child to understand that the old technique does not work any more. Parents have to be very strong and committed to what they are doing to get through this stage where things appear to be getting worse. On the positive side, you know the extinction method is working when the child starts to 'up the ante' on you. The behaviour will usually decrease gradually if you persist. *No* behaviour management method will provide instantaneous results.

Punishment

Punishment is a term used in behaviour management programmes that simply means that the child experiences something unpleasant after the behaviour has occurred. It is the opposite to receiving a reward or reinforcer.

In the past, some behaviour modification programmes used severe aversive treatment to punish, such as electric shock, and physical restraints to suppress behaviour, particularly for those children who had long histories of serious self-injury. Fortunately these aversive treatments have fallen from favour and new more humane approaches have taken their place, such as non-aversive 'gentle teaching' methods. Most people currently working with young children with autism and their families believe that severely aversive treatments have no place in behaviour management and education programmes today.

When working with young children with autism, two effective forms of punishment are still often used. They are not aversive, nor are they severe forms of punishment. These are: withdrawal and time-out. The child is punished only to the extent that he/she experiences something undesirable and not rewarding after a particular behaviour has occurred.

Withdrawal

Withdrawal refers to the removal or avoidance of a positive or pleasant experience. A typical example of withdrawal is the child who does not eat her dinner and as a result is sent to bed, so she misses out on TV and what the rest of the family is doing after dinner.

This method does rely on the child being aware of *why* he or she is being sent to bed and missing out, and for this reason it is not always useful with very young children or those who are unable to make the connection between the behaviour and the punishment. For those children who do understand the process it can be a very effective management strategy. It should not be used in a situation where the child does not understand why he/she is having a reinforcer withdrawn as this simply leads to complete bafflement in the child and no headway for the parents.

Time-out

Time-out is widely known and widely used to decrease undesirable behaviours. The idea here is that the child is removed from any sort of positive reinforcement after the undesirable behaviour has occurred. The underlying principle of time-out is that most people like to be rewarded with attention or some other positive feedback when a behaviour has occurred. If that behaviour is met with no positive reinforcement, and the child is actually removed from any opportunity for positive reinforcement, the behaviour is less likely to happen again.

Most people think that in order to put the child in 'time-out' he or she must be sent to another room and left alone. This is certainly one way of using the procedure, but it is not the only way.

Time-out can also occur by ignoring the child while he or she is still in the same room. If you like, it is time-out from Mum's attention. Time-out can also be very effective if the child is taken to a quiet area away from other activities and people in the same room.

It is important to have a specific time-out period that is not too long – five to ten minutes should be ample for a young child. If it has been necessary to remove the child from the room, you must ensure that he/she is safe from harm and you can hear what is going on.

Another approach is to send the child to time-out until they are ready to return and behave, but you must be prepared to keep sending the child back to time-out until they comply. One disadvantage with time-out is that it is not particularly 'portable' and is best used at home or a place that is familiar to both you and your child. For example it is difficult to time-out your child in the middle of the supermarket, although we have seen it tried.

The other thing to keep in mind about time-out is that for some children with autism, the removal to a quiet and empty space may actually be rewarding. We have seen children misbehave in classrooms with the sole purpose of being sent to the time-out area where they have happily sat doing nothing for half an hour. Time-out for children such as these is actually a positive reinforcer, so be careful.

Time-out can be effective as a 'circuit breaker' for both child and parent when a break or separation is needed to stop a situation from escalating. Time-out may also be used to provide an opportunity for the parent and child to cool down, and the parent to think through how best to respond.

It must be remembered that punishment methods suppress behaviour; they do not create anything in its place. Therefore they are best used in conjunction with methods that teach new or replacement behaviours.

No behaviour management programme should consist only of punishment procedures. There should be a balance between trying to reduce behaviour you do not want and encouraging new behaviour that you *do* want.

Teaching Mum how to behave: Matthew aged four

Matthew's mum reported:

> Matthew had been hitting his little sister. The consequence for this was that he was sent to his room. I was particularly cross with him this time and I smacked him on the bottom before he went to his room. I know I shouldn't...but I did. We also had a little behaviour script about not hitting his sister. I went into his room and read the script to him, going over the rule about not hitting anyone, and he turned to me and said: 'That's right Mum...no hitting, so don't hit me.'

A reward or a punishment? Timmy aged eight

A teacher reported:

> Timmy was travelling in the car with the teacher from home to a school holiday camp. It was a long journey of about three hours. Timmy had been quite restless and noisy so the teacher had suggested a little game of counting the number of cars and trucks that they passed to give him something to do. He loved to count and enjoyed this activity. He was doing very well, sitting quietly counting traffic and, as a reward, the teacher gave him a sherbet sweet. Well, he spluttered and coughed, his eyes watered and he began to cry. He *hated* the feeling of the sherbet fizzing in his mouth. What she had thought would be a pleasant reward for his good behaviour was more like a punishment and he took a great deal of settling down to recover from this unpleasant experience.
>
> Never assume that you know what a child with autism will find rewarding! It was a lesson that the teacher never forgot and it happened over 20 years ago.

Individual Session 4

How to change inappropriate behaviour by manipulating consequences

In this session, you will discuss how to reinforce behaviour and manipulate consequences. Find reinforcers that suit your child. What behaviours do you find unacceptable? How should you use punishment?

Tasks for this session

- Make a list of behaviours your child has that you think are inappropriate and *why* you think this.

- Make a list of things that you think your child would find rewarding (reinforcers). Try them out. What was the response?

- Have you ever tried punishing your child? What was the punishment and what happened afterwards?

Task 1: List any behaviours your child has that you think are inappropriate and why you think so

1. Inappropriate behaviour

    Why?

2. Inappropriate behaviour

    Why?

3. Inappropriate behaviour

    Why?

Task 2: List of rewards (reinforcers) and responses to them

Reward	Response

Task 3: Punishment tried and what happened after (response)

Type of punishment	What happened after?

Group Session 5

How to encourage new behaviour

| → Prompting | → Shaping | → Chaining |

Past experience has taught those in the field of educating and managing behavioural problems in young people with autism that it is not enough to simply remove an undesirable behaviour. The danger is that it will be replaced with another that may be more difficult than the one that was removed. Therefore, the approach to behaviour management that combines teaching children new skills together with the suppression of undesirable behaviours is preferable.

There are several ways of encouraging and increasing new behaviours. Three commonly used methods are: the use of prompts, shaping and chaining.

Prompting

This is a procedure that is used when the required behaviour does not exist at all. The child is guided to perform the response. There are a number of ways to prompt a child.

Physical prompts are literally 'hands on' attempts to encourage the new behaviour. For example, if the new behaviour required is for the child to eat using a fork rather than his fingers, the physical prompt will involve putting your hand over the child's on the fork and helping him to stab the food and lift it to his mouth.

Verbal prompts involve telling the child what to do. For example, 'Stab your food with the fork.' Verbal prompts need to be very explicit and concrete at first. It is not sufficient just to say 'Use your fork' as it does not tell the child exactly what they should be using their fork for (e.g. the child might use his fork very well to poke the cat).

Pointing can also be used to prompt the correct response. The idea of using prompts is that eventually the prompt will fade and become unnecessary over time.

At first a combination of prompts is usually required. For example, a physical prompt will be combined with a verbal prompt that clearly tells the child what to do as he is doing it. As the behaviour is improving, the physical prompt may be dropped and a point used with the verbal prompt instead.

We have seen very subtle prompts being used very successfully with older children where a new behaviour has been learnt but the child still needs just a little cue or reminder of what to do. For example, in the classroom, a child who continually shouted out to contribute enthusiastically to the class had to learn to put up his hand and wait for the teacher to say his name. The cue he continued to need was simply the teacher raising a finger to indicate that he needed to raise his hand. The benefit of a small cue is that it helps the child without being obvious to everyone else.

Shaping

Shaping is another commonly used method to teach a new behaviour. This method involves encouraging and reinforcing successive approximations of the new behaviour until the behaviour is learnt.

For example, if the child is unable to wave goodbye, any attempt to raise a hand or arm in response to your waving goodbye is rewarded. It may begin with only a slight movement. As the child gets better at raising her arm and moving her hand you wait until both occur before giving the reward. The child learns that more is expected of her in gradual steps until the whole wave is learnt.

Shaping is a useful method to use with young children at any developmental level. It does not require the child to have an existing level of speech or comprehension of speech. Shaping can be used without spoken instructions, although praise and encouragement through words usually accompany the reward. It does require some ability in the child to attend and imitate an action.

Chaining

This is a useful way of teaching a more complex behaviour or task and involves breaking it down into small steps. The steps are then taught one at a time. As each step is learnt, the next is taught. You cannot miss steps, or teach them out of logical order. You can chain either backwards or forwards, which sounds complicated, but is not.

Self-help skills, such as dressing, are often taught using this method – for example, pulling up pants. The task has a lot of different steps which need to be thought about and written down. If you are forward chaining, you start with the first step which may be picking the pants up in both hands. The next step may then be lifting one leg to step into the pants etc. If you are using backward chaining you teach the other way around and start with the last step which would be the final pulling up of the pants.

The trickiest part in chaining is probably sitting down and working out the steps involved. The good thing about chaining is that the task is broken down into tiny steps that do not overwhelm the child and you work through one step at a time until the whole task has been learnt. Success builds on success as each step is mastered.

This method is very successful when teaching young children with few skills and who also have little language.

Individual Session 5

How to encourage new behaviour

This is a practical session that explains how to use prompting, shaping and chaining to encourage new behaviours in your child.

Tasks for this session

- Can you think of three new behaviours or skills you would like your child to learn? Write them down.

- Together, we will develop a programme using prompting, shaping and chaining methods to encourage these new behaviours.

Task 1: New behaviours I would like my child to learn

1.

2.

3.

Group Session 6

Communication problems in autism in verbal children

Communication problems are present in *all* children with autism. It is one of the core symptoms that must be present if a child has the diagnosis of autism. Communication problems in children with autism present in a number of different ways with different outcomes according to the problem type and severity. Some children have such severe communication problems that they do not speak at all. Other children have very delayed and unusual speech that makes it difficult for them to make themselves understood. A smaller group of children have superficially better speech but have problems knowing how to use their language to communicate well with other people.

Because of the wide range of communication problems and how they affect children with autism, we will be looking at them in two parts. First, verbal children who have speech that is both disordered and delayed, and second, non-verbal children who have no speech and must be taught other ways to communicate.

Recently, more attention has been paid to the effects of communication problems on children's behaviour. It is therefore doubly important that parents understand the type and severity of the communication problems their child has. This is necessary in order to work out more effective ways of communication and also to find possible explanations of behavioural problems that may be linked with communication difficulties.

The first step is assessment. It is difficult to put appropriate intervention programmes (either language or behavioural) in place without careful assessment of the child's current level of cognitive and language functioning.

Verbal children

About 50 per cent of young children with autism will acquire functional speech. They will begin to speak later than is normal and speech will be acquired more slowly. It is common for them to have both delayed and disordered communication.

We discussed communication problems in autism in an earlier session and will return to these now. First, what is meant by 'functional speech'? Children with autism may learn to talk but may not use the language they have to communicate effectively. Parents of a young child with autism know just how different the speech of their child is. Let's look at some of the ways children with autism 'talk' (*expressive language*).

- Words may come very slowly and some may even disappear again.

- Words may come in chunks or complete sentences out of the blue.

- Echolalia, or the repeating of words and phrases, may be present in a number of forms. For example, the child may immediately repeat what you have just said to him. Echolalia may also be delayed, with the child repeating a word or phrase heard previously. Echolalia may also be mitigated, with the child using some repeated words but adding some of his own to try to get his message across.

- The same word or sound may be repeated over and over again.

- A word may be used completely out of context or a made-up word (a neologism) used for a particular object.

- Pronouns are often reversed and confused.

- Tone, pitch and modulation may be unusual. The child's voice may sound flat, may have an unusual accent or may be too loud or too soft.

There are usually also problems with the child's understanding of language. These are called *receptive language* or *comprehension* problems, such as:

- difficulty understanding the meaning of what others say

- difficulty understanding a sequence of instructions

- lack of understanding of metaphor, for example 'shake a leg'

- very literal use of language and interpretation of what others say, for example 'hang on', so they do.

There are also a range of difficulties that verbal children have with conversation. Children with autism usually have difficulty attending to the other person. Conversation relies on two people listening to each other and taking turns to speak. For children with autism, this is a particular problem. Although they may have useful speech, they do not speak *conversationally*. The child with autism is more likely to talk at you rather than with you. Initiating and sustaining a conversation are also areas of difficulty.

The more verbal child may have special topics he wants to talk about to the exclusion of all else even at inappropriate times, or he may bombard you with questions that no answer you give seems to satisfy and stop the questioning.

How do these language problems affect the behaviour of verbal children?

Problems with the child's use and understanding of language can affect behaviour in a number of ways. It is important to keep these communication problems in mind when trying to determine the cause of specific behaviour problems and include them in your thinking.

It is also important that others who come into contact with your child, such as family, friends, relatives and respite care workers, understand how your child communicates and how communication problems may be affecting his/her behaviour.

Some examples:

1. *Echolalia* may be irritating and annoying to listen to, but may serve a number of useful functions for the child. By repeating what has been said, the child may be indicating 'Yes', for example when he repeats 'Do you want a drink?' The echolalia may also be helping the child to understand what has been said to him by repeating the sentence and going over it out loud. For some children, echolalia increases in situations where they are tense and anxious and may be a sign to watch out for.

2. *Tone, pitch and modulation* can be problematic. For example, a child who speaks too loudly can upset others with loud comments. Put a loud voice together with a child who naively makes comments about people and the result can be embarrassing for everyone. This situation may be interpreted as the child being ill-mannered when it is, in fact, part of the problem of voice production and the social use of language.

3. *Poor comprehension* can mislead others into thinking a child is being uncooperative or cheeky. For example, a child with autism who is asked 'Can you pick up the paper?' may respond 'Yes' and simply stand there not realizing that you are asking him to pick up the paper now. Poor understanding or literal interpretation of what is said is common. If you want him/her to follow an instruction, it is better to state the request directly and unambiguously and then check to make sure that the child understands. Written instructions can be helpful and also the use of pictures may clarify things for the child.

4. *Literal interpretation of what others say* is yet another situation where the child's behaviour may appear to be smart or rude. An instance that I remember well was when working with a little boy on

some tabletop activities. I stood up and said 'Hang on, I'll get another puzzle', so he took me by the arm to hang on. We frequently use metaphor as well. Children can perplex teachers in busy classrooms by standing and shaking their legs or wriggling when the instruction to hurry up has been given as 'Get a wriggle on' or 'Shake a leg'.

5. *Repetitive and stereotyped speech* such as repetitive questioning can be very difficult to cope with. This may be occurring because the child actually wants to have a conversation but does not know how to go about it. What seems like annoying behaviour may be a lack of skill in initiating and sustaining a conversation. If this is the cause for the behaviour, then an effective response will be giving the child some help with conversation starters and topics. If you have wrongly assumed that the child is asking annoying questions simply to get your attention, ignoring him will either make the situation worse or quite possibly make him give up in his attempts to talk with you.

Higher-functioning children with more verbal skills can appear to be superficially quite competent. It is these children who can get into all sorts of trouble because they *appear* to be very competent. It is difficult for other people who do not know them well to understand that the child continues to have problems with understanding and use of language.

Taking things literally: Ryan aged five

Ryan's mother reported:

> Ryan got wet and muddy when he was playing outside in the back yard. I told him to take off his socks and put new ones on. A bit later I said: 'Ryan, put your socks in the washing machine please.'
>
> I went to the laundry to do the washing after lunch and when I lifted the lid on the washing machine I was surprised to see about 20 pairs of socks in there. Ryan had put *all* of his socks in the washing machine. I couldn't be cross, could I? He had done *exactly* what I said…he put his socks in the washing machine. Next time I'll remember to be more specific and say 'put your wet, muddy socks in the washing machine'.

Individual Session 6

Communication problems in autism in verbal children

Tasks for this session

- Complete the communicative means-functions questionnaire. This task may help give you some idea of how your child uses actions or words to express his or her needs or feelings.

- Make a list of communication problems you think your child has. We will talk about these during the session.

- Can you think of a *behavioural* problem your child has that may be linked to one of these *communication* problems?

Task 1: Communicative means-functions questionnaire (adapted from Quill 2000)

Some young children with autism have enough words to get their message across; others with very few words might have to show you what they want and children with no speech at all may only be able to communicate with you by doing something and you have to work out what it is they are trying to let you know. These questions may help you to think about how your child communicates with you.

What does your child do/say when he wants to:

1. get your attention?

2. get help?

3. eat or drink something?

4. indicate 'no'?

5. indicate 'yes'?

6. indicate 'had enough/stop/no more'?

7. comment about an object?

8. comment about making a mistake?

9. greet someone?

10. let you know he is feeling happy/sad/angry/hurt?

Task 2: List any communication problems you think your child has

1.

2.

3.

4.

Is one of these communication problems related to a behavioural problem? Why?

Group Session 7

Communication problems in autism in non-verbal children

Non-verbal children

Approximately 50 per cent of children with autism do not acquire functional speech. It is still not clear why this is so. Some argue that it is because children with autism have underlying social deficits and problems with joint attention. Others argue that it is because children with autism have a basic lack of understanding that people have thoughts and feelings that can be related to. Others suggest that there are functional deficits in parts of the brain that process language.

Whatever the cause, children who are non-verbal have to get their message across about their needs and desires to others in some way other than speech. Over recent years it has become increasingly clear that there is a significant link between the child's communication problems and behavioural difficulties.

How do these language problems affect the behaviour of non-verbal children?

Remember the old saying 'actions speak louder than words'? In the absence of speech, the child with autism may find that the most effective way of communicating is through an action. The action may not always be appropriate but is sure to be repeated if it gets the child what he or she needs.

For example, a child may scream loudly when she wants something to eat. She may have learnt from the time she was a baby that when she cried she was fed, and so the behaviour has continued to get the food she wants. For another child, the same behaviour, screaming, may be a means of getting attention or an offer of activity. This child may have learnt in the past that when he screams he is given something to do or play with to keep him quiet and so has learnt that this is a very effective way of actually asking for something to do. The challenge for parents and others is learning to interpret what the child means when they behave in a particular way.

Children can be taught how to have their needs met through using words, pictures or simple signs. We spoke in an earlier session of the recent work of some researchers who have been investigating the communicative function of disruptive behaviours in young children who are non-verbal. It is thought that non-verbal children use these behaviours to express a range of functions such as: to get help, to refuse goods/services, to get objects, activities and company, and to escape from stressful situations.

It is possible to explore how the child expresses his/her needs by watching carefully and completing a communicative intentions/functions checklist and building up a picture of how the non-verbal child gets his/her message across to others. Once the child's current methods of communication have been identified, this information can be used to plan ways in which different or more acceptable behaviours can be taught.

Improving non-verbal communication using augmentative systems

Follow-up studies have shown that for most children with autism who do not have useful speech by about the age of seven years, it is likely that their ability to communicate verbally will remain severely impaired. It is important for these children to have some form of augmentative communication system (Howlin 1998).

Augmentative communication helps children who do not have speech to communicate by using other systems. These systems are called 'augmentative' because they augment or increase the strength of the child's power to communicate.

Simple pictures and line drawings such as COMPIC or PECS, signing systems such as Makaton and also photographs are often used to augment communication for children with autism. Each child must be carefully assessed to determine which system will suit them best. The majority of children with autism have better developed visual recognition skills but have more delayed imitation skills. Therefore a picture-based system may be more suitable.

The choice of system to help improve the child's communication will depend upon his/her level of cognitive and language ability. We will look at three systems frequently used in communication programmes for children with autism.

Signing

Signing was probably the first alternate system used with non-verbal children with autism. At first, the signing systems used by the deaf were taught, but these are complex systems that require finger spelling of words and use abstract concepts.

In the early 1980s, a simpler system called Makaton was devised to use with children with intellectual disability. This system has varying degrees of difficulty, but at its earliest level, signs are simple, concrete and do not require difficult finger spelling. Many of the first signs use only one hand. For example, the sign for drink uses one hand in the shape of a cup that is lifted to the mouth and tilted as if the child were having a drink.

One advantage of signs is that they are very portable and do not require the child to carry around equipment. Another advantage of establishing a signing system is that it has been found to encourage speech in children contrasting to what some parents fear, that signing might reduce the chance of their child talking. However, signing is not widely understood in the community and the child may not always be well understood outside the circle of those who can sign with him/her. Signing also requires that the child attends to the person teaching the signs and is able to imitate an action.

COMPIC and PECS

COMPIC (1992) (computer generated pictures) are a communication resource developed in Australia by COMPIC and are successfully used in many teaching programmes. These pictures consist of simple and clear line drawings that represent a wide range of objects, actions and feelings. They can be used initially at a very simple but practical level with young children who learn to point at the picture or show the picture to indicate their needs. When children are familiar with a number of these pictures, they can be put into a wallet of pictures that the child carries with him/her and uses to indicate his/her needs. The child gradually builds up a vocabulary of pictures to meet his/her own special needs.

COMPIC programmes are widely available in both computer software and loose-leaf book formats. COMPIC pictures are easily understood by everyone and do not require the child to learn and remember complex actions, as does signing. Children who have low cognitive skills can generally use a picture system in a simple way to communicate more effectively.

The Picture Exchange Communication System (PECS) (Frost and Bondy 1994) is another augmentative communication system. Developed in the early 1990s, PECS is widely used in early intervention and school programmes to teach children how to initiate communication. An advantage of this system is that it does not require complex or expensive materials and can be used in a variety of settings by parents, carers and teachers. PECS begins with teaching a student to exchange a picture of a desired item with a teacher who immediately honours the request. Verbal prompts are not used. Once this step is mastered, the system goes on to teach discrimination of symbols and later simple 'sentences' are made from stringing together these symbols. Children can also learn to comment and answer direct questions using the PECS symbols.

Photographs and objects

Photographs of objects, activities and people in the child's world can also be used effectively with low-functioning children who cannot master the use of symbols or line drawings. Use of photographs usually requires that the child first learns to match an actual object with an exact photograph of the object. The child learns that the photograph represents the object. The photograph must be simple, clear and uncluttered. After the child has learnt to match photographs and objects, the more complex concept of matching photograph and activity or action can be taught.

Once the child is able to recognize a number of photographs, a photo vocabulary can be built up in the same way as a COMPIC vocabulary. Photographs can be used to help the child understand timetables or the steps involved in completing an activity. For example, the classroom may have photographs of the day's activities pinned to the wall. When each activity finishes, the child may put away that photograph. Similarly, when the child is required to get dressed, the steps involved may be pinned to his bedroom door in the correct sequence and easily followed.

Objects can be used in a similar way to photographs with children who have difficulty understanding photographs. Object timetables are useful. Objects that represent activities can be laid out or stuck on the wall to show the child what happens next. For example, a crayon means work at the table, and the next object is a juice box straw to indicate that snack time comes after work.

A great advantage of photographs and objects is that the child can attend to them for as long as he or she needs to, and also return to them to refresh his or her memory. This is not possible with a sign which is gone once it has been demonstrated.

How to encourage communication

There is no point in a child having communication skills she/he does not use. It can be a great challenge for parents and others to actually get the child with autism to use the skills they have to communicate with those around them.

Motivating children to communicate is the issue here. We know that children with autism lack motivation and the social desire to communicate with others. This is one of the basic deficits of autism. Our task is to make it worth their while to speak, sign or use pictures and objects with us.

The child with autism needs a strong incentive to communicate with others. If she/he manages to have a successful interaction with someone, it is more than likely to happen again. At the same time, if the child's attempts to communicate are ignored or unsuccessful, they can be turned off fast. ('Why bother to point to the picture of the juice if no one looks? I may as well just yell like I usually do.')

Communication does not occur in a vacuum. The child needs to have a *reason* and *something* to communicate. This applies whether the child has speech, signs, uses pictures or even objects to communicate. Look at the next section, 'Let's start communicating', for some ideas.

You can see that the ideas and activities here do a number of things. First, they remove the communication vacuum and provide activities which act as a focus for communication, for example looking at a book together. Second, they make communication fun and result in pleasurable experiences for the child, such as playing with toys. Third, they encourage children to communicate in order to get what they want by withholding an activity or making it necessary for the child to ask for help: For example, giving the child a jar of bubble mixture with its lid screwed on. The child needs to ask for help to open the jar before she can play with it.

Remember, having something to talk about or a reason to communicate is just as important as being able to communicate…for *all* of us.

Let's start communicating: Some ideas to get a communication interaction going in young children

- Activate a wind-up toy (e.g. a walking toy animal, spinning top etc.). Draw your child's attention to it and play with it together. Let it wind down. Wind it up and play again as before. Wind it up a third time and when it winds down do nothing. You are trying to motivate your child to keep the game going by indicating to you that he/she wants more. Give a prompt (verbal): 'Do you want more?' *Wait* for a response. At the slightest response from your child, even if it is eye contact, wind up the toy and play again. This gives the message that if your child communicates with you there will be a pay-off for them.

- Look at a book together. Talk about the pictures. Lift-the-flap books are good as you can try the 'wait for the response method' as in the game above.

- Blow some bubbles with a bubble wand and a jar of bubble mixture. Do this a few times then hand the jar to your child with the lid screwed on. Again you want to elicit a response and get your child to ask for help by indicating in whatever way they can. This may be thrusting the jar back at you or vocalizing or even saying 'more' or 'open please'.

- Put a favourite toy out of reach but in sight. Wait for a reaction.

- Play a game of rough and tumble or tickles. Stop and wait for your child to indicate, in whatever way they can, to keep the game going.

- Blow up a balloon. Let it go and watch it fly around the room and deflate. Pick it up and do it again. The third time, wait. Your child might go to get the deflated balloon and hand it to you to keep the game going.

Using photographs and offering choices: Jessica aged three and a half

Jessica's mum reported:

> Jessica and I were at the market buying fruit and vegetables. She likes to be out shopping and helps to carry things in the basket. She can't speak yet but she and I can understand each other most of the time and she uses photographs to show me what she wants.
>
> I took a basket, a new, bright red one, and started off down the aisle when Jessica began to scream and threw herself on the ground. I was a bit shocked and surprised because shopping is usually a happy time for us both. I was about to growl at her for being naughty but stopped and thought for a moment. Because I had been learning about ABC approaches to behaviour problems I stopped to think whether I had done anything to provoke this crying.
>
> Of course...I chose a different basket...we always have a blue basket at this shop. I bent down and showed Jessica the red basket and the blue basket and said, 'Which basket?', offering her a choice. She looked at me, then took the blue basket and put the red one back on the stack.
>
> We then took the blue basket and did the shopping. Next time we were at the market Jessica had photographs of the baskets and showed me which one she wanted by pointing to the photograph...yep, it was the blue one.

Communication problems in autism in non-verbal children

What are the implications of communication problems for you and your child?

Tasks for this session

- Have you tried any of the suggestions in the 'Let's start communicating' section? What happened?

- We will practise/discuss some of these ideas during the session with your child.

Group Session 8
Social impairment in autism

One of the key features of autism is difficulty with interpersonal relationships, such as: reduced responsiveness to or interest in people, an appearance of aloofness and a limited or impaired ability to relate to others, particularly their own age group.

Autistic infants often do not assume a normal anticipatory posture or put up their arms to be picked up and often do not seek physical comfort. However, they may show selective attachments to their primary caregivers. It is not simply the case that infants with autism do not develop social relating skills. It is more true to say that the quality of the relationship is abnormal.

Autistic children show very little variation in facial expression in response to others, generally have abnormal eye contact and tend not to spontaneously engage in social imitation such as waving goodbye and pat-a-cake games.

They rarely develop an age-appropriate empathy or ability to understand that other people have feelings. Their ability to make friends is absent or distorted and they are usually unable to play reciprocally with other children.

All children with autism have impaired social skills; however, the nature of these impairments can vary and may modify as the child grows older. For example, there may be an increase in interest in other people and the development of some social skills but these are usually learned and applied in a mechanical or inflexible manner.

Treatment

Social impairment in autism affects most aspects of the person's functioning (Howlin 1998). The approaches used to treat social difficulties vary according to the needs of each person with autism, particularly their level of cognitive ability, age and the nature of their social impairment.

For example, the young child with autism who is aloof and withdraws from social contact requires a very different programme to an older, more able adolescent who attempts to join in with others but shows little empathy or reciprocity.

There is a range of social difficulties which might be the focus of attention such as: understanding about friends and strangers, social play skills, interacting with peers, understanding rules and when they may be broken, understanding emotions and increasing imaginative and social imitative play.

Treatment approaches for young children

Treatment for young children with autism initially involves the teaching of social skills according to specific, inflexible rules that can be learnt in specific situations such as 'You do not touch people's legs at the bus stop'. Behaviour scripts involving photographs and line drawings, and simple social stories that reinforce the rules, are useful. These visual supports make communication and social information easier for the child to understand.

Treatment approaches for older children and adolescents

As children grow older social skills training may include the use of picture scripts and social stories at a more sophisticated level. Social skills training groups, role plays and outings offer adolescents other avenues for learning more appropriate social skills and provide opportunities to practise these skills *in situ*.

Social assistance

Carol Gray (1996) has developed an innovative approach to 'socially assist' young people with autism. This approach involves working together with the young person, respecting each individual's strengths and abilities rather than controlling the person's social behaviour, and comprises the following components.

1. *Picture scripts*: these are drawings that represent social situations and how to handle them and help the child rehearse social situations and learn a range of appropriate responses.

2. *Social stories*: these aim to help the child understand social situations, routines and make judgements about a social situation on an individual basis. Details are gathered about a problem situation (the target), the person's abilities, interests and responses, and others involved. These details are used to form a story. The person is given information about the situation and how to respond. Stories can be written, or presented as videotapes or audio tapes for those who cannot read.

3. *Comic strip conversations*: these are used with adolescents to clarify important interactions and describe appropriate social behaviour through the use of simple drawings.

4.   *Social review*: the adolescent and the therapist review a videotape of an actual situation to help understand the perspective of the adolescent with autism in an informal way, share accurate information and provide an opportunity to identify new responses to the situation.

5.   *Social skills groups*: this includes the involvement of non-autistic peers who can help teach social interaction skills. Role-play activities and videotapes are used to teach and practise social interaction skills and enable the person with autism to observe his/her behaviour and practise correct responses in a more naturalistic setting.

Not understanding 'niceness': James aged nine

James found a small box with a name on it when visiting his grandmother's house. He carried it into the lounge room and asked his grandmother: 'What's this?'

Grandmother replied: 'It's your grandfather's ashes.'

James: 'Can I take him to school for show and tell?'

Grandmother: 'No, that wouldn't be very nice, dear.'

James: 'We could put a hat and tie on him, and then he'd be nice.'

Individual Session 8

Social impairment in autism

What are the implications of social impairment for you and your child?

Tasks for this session

- Observe your child during the week.

- Do you think your child has problems with social skills? Some of the following may be useful to keep in mind:

    1. Is your child happiest 'doing his/her own thing' alone?

    2. Does he/she approach other children to join in with play activities? If yes, *how* is the approach made?

    3. Does he/she prefer to be with or make more approaches to adults?

    4. Are these approaches because he/she needs something or just to be sociable?

    5. What does your child do when visitors come to the house?

    6. What does your child do when a family member is upset?

    7. Is your child able to 'read' the signs as to how you may be feeling?

- Are there any particular social skills you would like your child to learn?

Task 1: Social problems I have observed

Task 2: New social skills I would like my child to learn

1.

2.

3.

Group Session 9

How to work and play together

→ The importance of play

→ How to gain your child's attention

→ To increase eye contact, attending and staying on task, remember...

Teaching children with autism to play is hard work. Hard work for the teacher (in this case you, the parents or carers) and hard work for the child who would generally much rather he/she be left alone to do his/her own thing. For this reason, this session is called working and playing together.

So far we have...

1. looked at how autism affects children's language and behaviour
2. discussed some of the ways of increasing communication skills in children who can talk and in those who are not yet talking
3. discussed aspects of the behavioural problems that many children with autism have and how we can bring about changes in these behaviour patterns by both decreasing inappropriate behaviour and at the same time teaching new behaviour
4. discussed aspects of social impairments that affect most children with autism and how we can promote and encourage better social relating skills.

Another important aspect of each child's development is the ability to fill in their day with useful activity and social contact. For most typically developing young children, the day is spent in a combination of activities involving relating to other children and adults in their world, eating, resting and, for many hours each day, playing.

This range of daily activities is *not* typical for the child who has autism.

Lack of creative and imaginative play is one of the diagnostic features of autism that we discussed earlier in the programme. The ability to play generally has to be taught and so, in a way, becomes *work* for children with autism. They may much prefer to spend their time engaged in rituals and repetitive routines that exclude social contact and interest in what is going on around them. These behaviours can become so entrenched that there is no time left for useful activity.

The importance of play

We now know that the earlier play skills can be taught to young children, the better the chance that rituals and routines may decrease. We also know that intrusion on the child's isolation is an important way of establishing contact. This can be done by offering toys and objects and establishing play routines and games that the child finds enjoyable.

Teaching the child to play, by themselves and with others, therefore serves a number of important functions:

- Children learn about their world through play.

- Children's ability to communicate relates to their ability to play symbolically. Improved play skills can lead to improved communication skills.

- As play skills increase, rituals and routines usually decrease.

- Interactive play can increase social skills such as learning to take turns, sharing, and co-operating.

- Play with toys provides an opportunity to teach the child new skills that are important for later formal education. Some examples are: attending to others, attention to task, turn-taking, following instructions, and opportunities and topics for conversation.

We will now look at how some of these skills may be developed through play.

How to gain your child's attention

How to be intrusive

It is important to intrude upon the autistic child's isolation. However, there are ways of doing this that are more successful than others. Intrusion for no reason other than to gain your child's attention will not be very rewarding for your child or you. It is possible to intrude in a way that is gentle, persuasive and also interesting for your child, but it does take practice.

If we want children to be less isolated then it follows that the contact they have with others needs to be pleasant and rewarding for them. If the result of our intrusion on children is neither pleasant nor rewarding for them, we will probably achieve the opposite and turn them even further away from us.

You are more likely to intrude successfully by offering your child something to look at or do. This is where play and toys come into the picture. Intruding, by offering a toy to play with, provides the opportunity to gain your child's attention and start some pleasant interaction.

Intruding through the offer of a toy and then teaching your child how to play with that toy opens a wider range of possibilities for further interaction and involvement together.

Teaching eye contact and attending to task and others

Eye contact between people is important.

- It establishes a connection between people.

- It is a means of letting the other person know that you are attending to what they have to say.

- A child cannot learn if he/she is not looking or attending.

- It is necessary to attend to an instruction before it can be learnt (e.g. learning signs).

There are lots of ways to encourage eye contact and attention. Here are some suggestions:

1. Get down to the same level as your child.
2. Say your child's name and touch him if necessary to get his attention.
3. Say 'Look at me' before you say anything else.
4. Gently touch your child's chin to orient his face to your face.
5. Point to your eyes when you are telling your child to look at you.
6. Hold toys or food or whatever you have for him up at your face level to encourage him to look up and attend to your face, rather than down.
7. Always tell him when he's got it right: 'Good looking.'

Staying on task

Having gained the child's attention and eye contact, it is then important to keep it going. Children must be able to attend for learning to take place.

If your child cannot sit and attend to you and your instruction, it is unlikely that you will have any success with teaching new tasks.

For example, if your child cannot attend and copy a simple body movement such as raising her arms above her head, she will be unable to imitate more complex actions required in sign language. This would then indicate that you need to work further on basic attention before you can progress to shaping new behaviours.

Staying on task can be learnt and improved upon with practice. Play is an ideal way of creating an activity to teach this skill to young children.

Many school tasks require attentional skills. It is far more difficult for a school-aged child to have to begin learning about attending and staying on task when he starts at school than learning them at an early age through play.

Here are some suggestions:

1. Start with an activity that has a definite finishing point, for example a one-piece puzzle. Put in the piece together and the task is complete and your child is ready for a reward. Attention to task can be increased by making the task longer, for example

gradually build up to a ten-piece puzzle and you have increased your child's attention for that activity by ten.

2. Stay away from open-ended activities that have no definite end point, for example painting which can go on for as long as the child likes, or be done as quickly as the child likes, such as in a couple of seconds.

3. If things are getting bogged down, use modelling and hands-on assistance to complete the activity together so that you can give a reward quickly and keep your child motivated and feeling successful.

4. Talk your way through the task. Say it as you do it, for example 'Push the button'.

5. Use simple, clear language, and not too many words.

To increase eye contact, attending and staying on task, remember...

- Regular practice is essential and incidental teaching should become a part of your daily routines and activities.

- It will become automatic for all of you if you follow the suggestions often enough.

- Use simple, clear language or a picture that tells your child *what to do*, not what not to do.

- Always praise your child when he/she gets it right.

Individual Session 9

How to work and play together

This section explains how to intrude, teach eye contact and help your child to stay on task.

Tasks for this session

- This session is about being intrusive, working on eye contact and teaching your child how to stay on task by playing together.

- Together, we will develop a programme to work on these skills through activities that suit both you and your child at a pace that is practical for everyone.

Group Session 10

Review and critique of programme – where next?

This final group session provides an opportunity to go over what we have covered during the previous 18 sessions together. The final individual session will also provide this opportunity in a more personal way for each of you.

For this reason, today the discussion does not have a specific outline and direction beyond picking up on issues that you yourselves raise. You may like to look back over the group sessions and discuss the aspects that you found most helpful. You may like to discuss the possibilities of staying together as a support group when the programme is over.

Your manual has been added to each week with ideas and practical suggestions from your homework tasks and you now have information on a wide range of issues about autism as well as some related to parenting young children with disabilities in general. We hope that you will refer to this manual and the ideas it contains. There may have been some information that is not all that relevant for you and your child at the moment but in a year or two you may well find that the teaching strategies and behaviour management ideas come in handy as your child develops, learns and grows.

Individual Session 10

Review and critique of programme – where next?

Tasks for this session

As this is our last session together in this part of the programme, it will be an opportunity for you to raise any outstanding issues, reflect on what we have discussed and done together and talk about what happens next.

- The parent feedback forms should be returned during this session (if relevant).

- Appointments for any follow-up assessments/sessions will also be made today (if relevant).

Appendix 1
Useful Websites and Further Reading

Websites

Autism

www.autismvictoria.org.au
www.nas.org.uk
www.autism.org.au
www.autism-society.org
www.autism-resources.com
www.autism-pdd.net

Coping with grief and stress

www.coping.org/copingbook/griefloss.htm
www.autism-society.org (Stress on Families Article)

Managing behaviour

www.nas.org.uk (Understanding Behaviour Fact Sheet)
www.autism.org.au/BEHAVIOUR%20MANAGEMENT.htm
www.do2learn.com

Communication

www.nas.org.uk (The Use of Picture Symbols Fact Sheet)
www.comeunity.com/disability/speech/autism.html (Communication in Autism)
www.ttac.odu.edu/articles/autism.html (Communication and Behaviour Links Article)
www.autism.org/temple/visual.html (Article about an autistic person's experiences of sensory and communication difficulties)
www.nidcd.nih.gov/health/voice/autism.asp (Information about autism and communication)

Social skills

www.polyxo.com/socialstories/introduction.html (Social Stories)
www.udel.edu/bkirby/asperger/social.html
www.arlington.k12.va.us/schools/jamestown/classrooms/mipa/skills.html

Play

www.nas.org.uk (Play and Autism Fact Sheet)
www.do2learn.com (activities, worksheets, craft ideas)

Sibling issues

www.autism-society.org (Sibling Issues Article)

Dietary issues

www.autism-society.org

Toilet training

www.isn.net/~jypsy/toileting.htm

Sensory difficulties

www.autism.org/temple/faq.html

Recommended books

General reference books and management guides for parents

Dickinson, P. and Hannah, L. (1998) *It Can Get Better – A Guide for Parents and Caregivers.* London: The National Autistic Society. (Practical information for handling common day-to-day problems.)

Howlin, P. (1998) *Children with Autism and Asperger Syndrome: A Guide for Practitioners and Carers.* Chichester: John Wiley and Sons. (An excellent overview of what autism is and includes management and teaching strategies.)

Morton-Cooper, A. (2004) *Health Care and the Autism Spectrum.* London: Jessica Kingsley Publishers. (An interesting book for parents and health professionals.)

Parents' accounts

Claiborne Park, C. (2001) *Exiting Nirvana: A Daughter's Life with Autism.* London: Arum. (Claiborne Park eloquently tells of her '40-year journey' with her daughter Jessy.)

Waites, J. and Swinbourne, H. (2001) *Smiling at Shadows.* Pymble, NSW: HarperCollins. (A description of family life with a Dane who was diagnosed with autism over 25 years ago as told by his caring parents.)

Siblings and family issues

Davies, J. (1993/4) *Children with Autism – A Booklet for Brothers and Sisters.* Nottingham: University of Nottingham. (Suitable for children in primary school.)

Harris, S. (1994) *Siblings of Children with Autism: A Guide for Families.* New York: Woodbine House. (An interesting book for parents to help them understand autism and sibling relationships.)

Siegel, B. and Silverstein, C. (1994) *What About Me? Growing Up with a Developmentally Delayed Sibling.* New York: Insight Books (Suitable for parents and older siblings.)

Books for children

Band, E. and Hecht, E. (2001) *Autism Through a Sister's Eyes.* Arlington, TX: Future Horizons. (Suitable for siblings and peers aged six and over.)

Bleach, F. (2001) *Everybody is Different.* London: The National Autistic Society. (This book explains autism in a simple way for young children aged six and over.)

Twatchman-Cullen, D. (1998) *Trevor, Trevor.* Cromwell, CT: Starfish Press. (A lovely book about a boy with autism at school and his helpful teacher. Suitable for children aged five and over.)

Autobiographical accounts
Grandin, T. and Scariano, M. (1986) *Emergence: Labelled Autistic.* Navato, CA: Arena Press. (The first 'inside narrative' of autism from Temple Grandin who was diagnosed with autism as a young child.)

Grandin, T. (1995) *Thinking in Pictures.* New York: Vintage Books. (Grandin gives a fascinating account of the workings of her visual mind, her life and love of animals.)

Appendix 2

Autism and Asperger's Disorder

Autism

What is autism?

Autism is a syndrome consisting of a set of developmental and behavioural features that must be present for the condition to be diagnosed.

The core features of autism include impairment in three main areas of functioning:

1. social interaction
2. communication
3. play and behaviour (restricted, repetitive and stereotyped patterns of behaviour, interests and activities).

(American Psychiatric Association 1994)

Kanner first described these core features in his paper of 1943 in which 11 children with 'autistic disturbances of affective contact' showed a distinctive pattern of symptoms:

1. inability to relate to people and situations
2. failure to use language for the purpose of communication
3. obsessive desire for the maintenance of sameness in the environment.

(Kanner 1943)

The DSM-IV (American Psychiatric Association 1994) diagnostic system emphasizes that symptoms may change throughout life and behaviour problems can range from severe to mild impairments.

What causes autism?

The cause of autism is unknown. It is a biological condition probably due to a number of causes acting together rather than one specific cause. It becomes obvious within the first 30 months of life. Autism affects the person throughout life.

SOME HISTORY

In the 1950s and early 1960s some (e.g. Bettelheim 1967) argued that autism was a schizophrenic withdrawal from reality and advocated residential centres for children, removing them from their families. Cold and rejecting parents were said to be causing autistic behaviour in their children and residential programmes were seen as a means of undoing autistic behaviours and establishing appropriate behaviours in their place. The treatment involved individual psychotherapy with the autistic child and attempts were made to change the parents and make them acknowledge their role in the development of the child's condition. Bettelheim (1967) referred to such a child as the 'empty fortress'. This 'psychogenic' theory and its treatment approaches fell from favour because it was not supported by evidence from systematic studies.

In the 1970s, new research highlighted basic cognitive deficits and organic brain dysfunction. This became known as the 'nature' theory of causation of autism and the bulk of the evidence pointed to a neurological (brain) dysfunction in autistic children.

Support for genetic influences on autism came from the research by Folstein and Rutter (1977), who undertook a study of 21 pairs of same-sex twins, one or both of whom had autism. This study pointed to the 'importance of brain injuries, especially during the perinatal period which may operate either by themselves or in combination with a genetic disposition involving language. Both mode of inheritance and exactly what is inherited remain uncertain.'

RECENT BRAIN RESEARCH

It is assumed that people with autism probably share certain common features of abnormal brain function, but the nature of this underlying neural pathology remains elusive and controversial.

Varied findings suggest that autism is a disorder that encompasses both sub-cortical and cortical levels of brain processing. Abnormal brain activity, arousal levels, deficits in the ability to respond accurately to sensory input, abnormal event related potentials measured in the brain, impairment of left hemisphere functioning, pathophysiology of the temporal lobe and specific structural abnormalities have been investigated.

Current research points to abnormalities in brain systems that are sub-served by brain stem structures such as the cerebellum and limbic system and there is evidence that the brains of people with autism are often underdeveloped and immature. Other researchers have reported increased head circumference and brain volume but these findings have not been linked to clinical features such as severity of autism or IQ levels.

Neurotransmitters such as serotonin have also been implicated, but abnormalities that have been found have not been shown to be specific to autism and the only consistent finding is the elevation of whole blood serotonin levels in about 25 per cent of individuals with autism. The significance of this is unclear, although Bailey, Phillips and Rutter (1996) suggested that developmental mechanisms in the brain may be affected.

Current neurobiologic theories postulate single or multiple primary clinical deficits in higher-order cognitive processing abilities, for example involving language, social understanding and emotional insight; and the involvement of the cerebral cortex in the final common pathway for the clinical symptomatology.

Future research is needed to define:
1. the pathophysiology of the clinical syndrome of autism
2. the developmental pathophysiology of the structural and functional brain abnormalities that underlie the clinical syndrome
3. the genetic mechanisms that trigger the disruption in brain development that lead to these abnormalities.

RECENT GENETIC RESEARCH

There is now no doubt that genetic factors play an important, if not central, role in the causation of autism although the precise genetic mechanisms have not been determined. Recent genetic research has attempted to address the issues of transmission of vulnerability to autism and the nature of the autistic phenotype. Evidence points to not a single gene but the interaction of at least three abnormal gene sites and perhaps as many as ten.

Autism is three to four times more common in males. The chance of having a first child with autism is less than 1:1000 but reduces to probably about 1:50 with a second child, particularly if it is male. There is also the increased likelihood of a family history of learning problems, speech delays, aloofness and social eccentricity, obsessional behaviours and depression.

It is anticipated that advancement in molecular genetics will help in the understanding of how the genes involved lead to autism, whether there is an interaction between specific environmental features and genetic susceptibility and why there is variation in the cognitive impairment that is associated with autism. Research concerning the genetic and environmental causes of autism continues; however, research findings are unlikely to translate into practical help for some time yet.

WHAT WE NOW KNOW ABOUT CAUSES OF AUTISM

Research over the past 40 years has clarified a number of issues about the causes of autism. The psychogenic causation theory of the 1950s has been found to be lacking in evidence and dismissed. Evidence has made it clear that autism is a neurodevelopmental disorder involving basic cognitive and information processing deficits, affect, communication and social skills. However, many questions remain unanswered regarding the neuropathophysiology of autism and the mode of genetic inheritance.

ASSOCIATED MEDICAL CONDITIONS

There is a frequent association between autism and a number of medical conditions that affect the brain, such as:

- pre- and perinatal trauma, neonatal asphyxia

- certain acquired encephalopathies and brain malformations

- metabolic disorders such as histidinemia, and Lesch-Nyhan syndrome

- genetic conditions and chromosomal abnormalities including Fragile X, tuberous sclerosis, Cornelia de Lange syndrome, Joubert syndrome, Williams syndrome and Hypomalanosis of Ito.

Most importantly, there is an approximately 30 per cent risk of developing seizures through childhood to early adulthood. The majority of persons with autism have non-specific abnormal electrical brain activity shown on an electro-encephalogram (EEG).

Some other medical conditions that lead to intellectual disability are rarely associated with autism, noticeably Down syndrome and cerebral palsy.

The nature and meaning of the association between autism and these various other neurobiological conditions has yet to be determined.

Diagnosing autism

Because the cause of autism is unknown, diagnosis relies upon matching the child's behaviour patterns and development with the diagnostic criteria. Autism usually emerges in early infancy, and the diagnosis of autism can be reliably made from two years of age.

In 1980, the American Psychiatric Association's *Diagnostic and Statistical Manual* (DSM-III) introduced the diagnostic term pervasive developmental disorder (PDD) to cover a group of disorders of development including autism which presented with abnormalities and impaired functioning across the social, cognitive, emotional and language domains. These impairments were present from the first few years of life.

The DSM-IV (American Psychiatric Association 1994) includes five categories of pervasive developmental disorders (PDDs):

- Autistic disorder (autism)

- Asperger's disorder (see p.104)

- Rett's disorder

- Childhood disintegrative disorder

- Pervasive developmental disorder – not otherwise specified (PDD-NOS).

RETT'S DISORDER

This is a progressive developmental disorder that appears primarily in girls. It is usually associated with severe intellectual disability. Development in infancy is normal; however, head circumference growth decelerates after about six months. Fine motor skills acquired earlier are gradually lost between the ages of six months to four years and are replaced with an obsessive hand wringing movement. There is also a gradual loss of gross motor function as lower limbs and trunk are affected. Children also gradually lose language skills, social interest and an interest in their environment. It is this aspect of the progressive disorder that may initially appear to be like symptoms of autism. Over the course of the disorder, children may become more socially aware, make more effort to communicate and make more eye contact than a child with autism. In adolescence girls have muscle wasting, scoliosis (curvature of the spine), spasticity and loss of mobility. Prevalence rate is about 1 per 20,000 (Tidmarsh and Volkmar 2003).

CHILDHOOD DISINTEGRATIVE DISORDER (ALSO KNOWN AS HELLER'S SYNDROME)

This is a very rare disorder with a prevalence rate of about 1.7 per 100,000, affecting males more often than females (Tidmarsh and Volkmar 2003). Development of language, social and play skills is normal for the first two to four years of life followed by regression without any associated medical cause. In most cases no specific neuropathological process is identified. To meet DSM-IV diagnostic criteria, a child must show regression in two of the following developmental areas: language, social, play or motor skills, adaptive behaviour, bowel or bladder control. The deterioration should occur before the age of ten years.

This diagnosis is used when other diagnostic criteria are not met. For example, children who do not fit diagnostic criteria because of age of onset or who do not have the key symptoms described for other PDD diagnoses. This category is somewhat open to interpretation by clinicians because of the lack of clear criteria. Despite this it is generally used to describe children such as those who may have global developmental delay and some symptoms of autism, or who fail to meet the strict criteria for autism. Children diagnosed with PDD-NOS must meet the criteria for severe and pervasive impairment in: reciprocal social interaction associated with impaired verbal or non-verbal communication skills or with the presence of stereotyped behaviour, interests and activities (DSM-IV, American Psychiatric Association 1994).

See *Diagnostic and Statistical Manual of Mental Disorders*, 4th Edition, 1994, Washington DC: American Psychiatric Association, pp. 70–71, for the specific diagnostic criteria.

AUTISM SPECTRUM DISORDERS

The term autism spectrum disorders (ASD) is currently used but its definition lacks the level of international agreement attached to pervasive developmental disorders.

For some, ASD refers to a group of different autistic-like conditions, a similar concept to PDD. For others, ASD refers to a unitary concept of autism conveying a notion of severity from the aloof intellectually delayed child with 'Kanner' type autism at the severe end through to intelligent, less severely disturbed children with Asperger's disorder (AS) at the other end of the spectrum.

The problem with this approach relates to what is being defined as severe to mild. Is it IQ level, or language ability, or obsessional behaviour, or social impairment? Young people with AS may have the intelligence on IQ testing of a typical child but might have severe impairment in social behaviour and crippling obsessions. Therefore, the concept of severity relates to multiple cognitive, social and behavioural domains and has limited if any value if applied to a child with PDD.

There is now a general international consensus regarding the development of features and behaviours that are required to make a diagnosis of autism defined in either the *International Classification of Diseases*, Tenth Edition (ICD-10) (World Health Organisation 1992) or the DSM-IV.

How common is autism?

Prevalence estimates for autism have been gathered for over 30 years. At least 23 prevalence studies have been reported in the literature from 1966 to 1997. These studies use varying diagnostic criteria as definitions of autism have changed over time and population samples have varied in size and type. The autism rate for studies published between 1966 and 1991 was 4.4 per 10,000. Recent works with the most rigorous ascertainment methods have consistently yielded rates of about 10 per 10,000 (Fombonne 2003). It has been suggested that the prevalence of autism is increasing; however, improved community awareness and assessment, together with changes in diagnostic practice, may have increased the number identified. Study design and methodology may also be contributing to increased prevalence rates in some cases. The prevalence rate for unspecified PDDs and PDD-NOS is 15 per 10,000. Fombonne's (2003) estimate for all 'autism spectrum disorders' is 27.5 per 10,000.

Reports of autism 'outbreaks' raise the question as to whether autism might be the result of some environmental risk or other factors. There have been reports of links between the onset of autism and the administration of the MMR (measles, mumps, rubella) vaccination. Several recent studies have found no association. The link between MMR and autism has not been confirmed by any robust study to date. Tidmarsh and Volkmar (2003) recently discussed the controversy regarding high levels of mercury in children with autism and the use of thimerosol in vaccines. The hypothesis is that the neurotoxic effects of mercury produce neurodevelopmental problems in vulnerable children. There is no evidence that children exposed to mercury from any source have a higher rate of autism. Furthermore, thimerosol was removed from vaccines in the US, Japan and Canada in the early 1990s yet prevalence rates of autism have been reported to have risen since that time.

What about social class, race or gender?

Fombonne (2003) reports that recent epidemiological studies have failed to support Kanner's early theory that social class and level of parental education was associated with autism. Rates of autism are similar throughout the world with no higher prevalence reported in any particular racial group. Autism is approximately four times more common in boys than girls. Despite this striking male predominance, there has been no research evidence to account for this sex ratio but it might point to an X chromosome link.

Assessment

It is clear from the DSM-IV diagnostic criteria that the diagnosis requires a comprehensive, multidisciplinary assessment comprising at least:

- developmental and family history

- observation of the child's behaviour and interaction with others

- a medical assessment including tests for known causes of developmental delay (e.g. chromosome analysis) and hearing tests

- a cognitive assessment using appropriate tests such as the Psychoeducational Profile–Revised (PEP-R) (Schopler *et al.* 1990) and the Wechsler Pre-school and Primary Scale of Intelligence–Revised (WPPSI-R) (Wechsler 1989)

- structured language assessment

- structured assessment tools such as the Autism Diagnostic Instrument and Observational Scales (Le Couteur *et al.* 1989; Lord *et al.* 1989), clinician completed rating scales such as the Childhood Autism Rating Scale (CARS) (Schopler *et al.* 1980), and parent or teacher completed checklists such as the Developmental Behaviour Checklist (DBC) (Einfeld and Tonge 1992)

- comprehensive and sensitive feedback to the parents and carers about the diagnosis as the first step in developing a plan of intervention and services required.

ASSESSMENT INSTRUMENTS

Over the past 40 years various instruments have been developed specifically to assist in the diagnosis of autism and measurement of associated behaviours.

Because the cause of autism is unknown, diagnosis relies heavily upon behavioural description, observation of the child's behaviour patterns and history of development being matched with the diagnostic criteria. Therefore assessment instruments assist in the screening for autism, standardization of diagnosis and measurement of change.

Contemporary assessment instruments are usually administered in one of three ways: a checklist or rating scale completed by a trained clinician based on behavioural observation, such as the Childhood Autism Rating Scale (Schopler *et al.* 1980), or the Autism Behaviour Checklist (Krug, Arick and Almond 1980); a structured parent/carer interview administered by a trained clinician, such as the Autism Diagnostic Instrument and Observational Scales (Le Couteur *et al.* 1989; Lord *et al.* 1989); or a parent/carer completed questionnaire, such as the Developmental Behaviour Checklist (Einfeld and Tonge 1992) or the Autism Screening Questionnaire (Berument *et al.* 1999).

No one instrument is able to undertake all the tasks of diagnosis, behavioural description, measurement of response to treatment or change over time, and serve as a screening instrument. At present clinicians and researchers must evaluate an instrument's ability to meet a specific purpose and choose the appropriate psychometrically sound instrument(s) from the range available.

EARLY SCREENING AND DIAGNOSIS IN YOUNG CHILDREN

Early detection of autism is important and there has been recent interest in identifying the characteristics of autism in very young children. We know from parent report and video footage that symptoms of autism are apparent within the first 24 months of a child's life. Autism can be reliably diagnosed in children from the age of two years (Volkmar *et al.* 2004). Developmental changes in the symptoms of autism are not well understood and may be affected by variability in cognitive impairments and the age of the child. For example, there have been reports that repetitive behaviours are less common in very young children with autism and that social abnormalities increase with age during childhood.

The severity of the condition, its prevalence and the effectiveness of early intervention provide good reasons for trying to detect autism earlier rather than later. A number of screens for the early detection of autism are available. The Checklist for Autism in Toddlers (CHAT) (Baron-Cohen, Allen and Gillberg 1992) is probably the best known screen to date and has been evaluated in a general population. It is designed for use with toddlers aged 18 months and comprises nine questions of the parent/carer and five direct observations of the child by a health professional. According to the CHAT, three key items are predictive of autism: protodeclarative pointing (pointing to show someone something), gaze monitoring and pretend play. Early screen instruments need to be approached with caution as they currently tend to have high miss rates, meaning that children who are screen-negative cases who potentially are misclassified and may then be excluded from specialist services.

Early identification of autism is a research priority as cost effective, early identification and referring children quickly to appropriate diagnostic services and then into early intervention programmes is indicated. The experience of many parents to date is that there is a considerable time lag between their first concerns about their child being noted, assessment completed and diagnosis made and early intervention commenced.

How does autism affect children?

SOCIAL IMPAIRMENTS

One of the key features of autism is abnormality in interpersonal relationships, such as reduced responsiveness to or interest in people, an appearance of aloofness and a limited or impaired ability to relate to others.

Infants with autism do not assume a normal anticipatory posture or put up their arms to be picked up and often do not seek physical comfort. However, they do show selective attachments to their primary caregivers. It is not simply the case that infants with autism do not develop social relating skills. It is more true to say that the quality of the relationship is abnormal.

Children with autism show very little variation in facial expression in response to others, generally have abnormal eye contact and tend not to engage in social imitation such as waving goodbye and pat-a-cake games.

They rarely develop an age-appropriate empathy or ability to understand that other people have feelings. Their ability to make friends is absent or distorted and they are usually unable to play reciprocally with other children. All children with autism show social impairments; however, the nature of these impairments can vary and may modify as the child grows older. For example, there may be an increase in interest in other people and the development of some social skills often learned in a mechanical or inflexible manner.

COMMUNICATION SKILLS

Impairments in both verbal and non-verbal communication skills are often the cause for parents of children with autism to be first concerned and seek help.

Children with autism usually have markedly delayed and disordered speech with approximately half failing to develop functional speech. Research supports the notion that approximately 50 per cent of children with autism will eventually have useful speech. Children with autism also have an impaired ability to use gesture and mime.

In those children who do develop language, the pattern of development and usage is strikingly odd. Tone, pitch and modulation of speech is often odd and the voice may sound mechanical and flat in quality with a staccato delivery. Some children speak in whispers or too loudly, sometimes developing an unusual accent.

Their understanding of spoken language is often literal and they fail to comprehend underlying meaning and metaphor such as 'shake a leg', or 'pull your socks up'.

Abnormal use of words and phrases is a common symptom of autism. Echolalia (repetition of language spoken by others) is one of the most noticeably unusual aspects of speech. It can be either the immediate repetition of what has just been said, or the delayed repetition of phrases. Some children repeat advertising jingles or large pieces of dialogue, perhaps days later, from videos for no apparent reason. Echolalic speech may serve some function.

Children with autism often confuse or reverse pronouns. Kanner originally attributed this to echolalia; however, more recent research has found that this problem relates to the deficits that autistic children have in understanding the perspective of another, joint attention and difficulty conceptualizing the notion of self and other.

Some children have idiosyncratic speech and neologisms such as 'door go by' when asking to go outside, or calling a drink a 'dorfla'.

Language comprehension (receptive language) deficits in autism are also of great importance. Poor understanding is probably linked to social difficulties and impairments in social understanding. Inability to express needs by words or gesture, or a significant difference in the child's ability to use words compared to their level of understanding of the verbal responses of others, is a source of frustration and can cause distress or disturbed behaviour.

Even those children with autism who develop a wide vocabulary and expressive verbal skills show difficulty with the pragmatic or social use of language. They have impaired ability to initiate conversation, communicate reciprocally with others and maintain the 'to and fro' of a conversation. The child with autism is more likely to talk at you rather than with you, to intrude and talk out of context and use speech as a means to an end rather than engage in a social conversation. Howlin (1998) described the 'failure to use communication for social purposes' as the most characteristic feature of the language deficit in autism.

PLAY AND IMAGINATION

Children with autism usually have rigid and limited play patterns with a noticeable lack of imagination and creativity. They may repetitively line up toys, sort by colour, or collect various objects such as pieces of string, special stones or objects of a certain colour or shape. Intense attachment to these objects can occur with the child showing great distress if these objects are taken away or patterns disrupted.

Older children may develop play that superficially appears to be creative, such as re-enacting the day at school with dolls and teddies, or acting out scenes from favourite videos. Observation of this type of play over time often reveals a highly repetitive, formalized scenario that does not change and cannot be interrupted.

Children with autism rarely involve other children in their play unless they are given a particular role in a controlled situation. Howlin (1998) drew a parallel between the pervasiveness of the language disorder in autism and the child's inability to develop normal, imaginative play patterns. The stereotypies seen in language are also observed in the repetitive, non-social and ritualistic play of children with autism.

RITUALISTIC AND STEREOTYPED INTERESTS OR BEHAVIOURS

Ritualistic and compulsive phenomena are also common, such as touching compulsions and rigid routines for daily activities. There is often an associated resistance to change in routine or the environment so that the child may become extremely distressed if, for example, a new route is taken going to school, the furniture in the house is rearranged, or the child is asked to wear new clothes.

Hand and finger mannerisms and repetitive complex body movements of a stereotyped kind such as hand flapping or tip toe walking are common. There is often a fascination with movement of objects such as spinning a plate or wheel. Close visual scrutiny of the fine detail of an object such as the edge of a table or pattern of spokes on a wheel is common, as is the collection of objects such as buttons or twigs. Many children with autism, especially in middle to late childhood, have unusual preoccupations that they follow often to the exclusion of other activities. These may involve a fascination with bus routes or train timetables in association with repeatedly asking questions to which specific answers must be given.

ASSOCIATED FEATURES

Many other abnormalities are associated with autism such as unusual dietary habits, sleep disturbance, abnormalities of mood and self-injurious behaviour. Perceptual abnormalities such as lack of response to pain, heightened sensitivity to sound and preoccupation with tactile stimulation are also common. These associated features are not specific to individuals with autism and may occur in other children with intellectual disability.

COGNITIVE ABILITIES AND IQ SCORES

Although Kanner stated that children with autism possessed normal cognitive potential and 'islets of ability', it is now quite clear that the majority of children with autism have intellectual disability.

In most epidemiological samples approximately 50 per cent of cases exhibit severe intellectual disability, 30 per cent mild to moderate disability and the remaining 20 per cent have IQs in the normal range. Low IQ scores are more likely to be associated with the development of epilepsy. One third of intellectually disabled children with autism develop epilepsy whilst only approximately one in 20 of those with normal intelligence do.

IQ scores of children with autism often show an unusual and distinctive pattern of performance on standardized tests of intelligence.

Individual profiles usually show a wide scattering of abilities with deficits in verbal sequencing and abstraction skills, although rote memory may be relatively better. Tasks requiring manipulative, visuo-spatial skills or immediate memory may be performed well, such as Block Design, Object Assembly and the Seguin Formboard. These skills may be the basis of 'islets of ability' such as musical ability shown by a few children with autism. Around 20 per cent of children with autism have overall cognitive abilities in the normal range and are referred to as 'high-functioning', but still usually have the pattern of a relatively wide scattering of abilities.

The cognitive deficit is as much social as intellectual and linguistic. Rutter (1983) contended that these cognitive deficits are basic to the condition of autism and not secondary features. It has been found that such deficits are present in virtually all children with autism and that they constitute the most powerful predictors of functioning in later adolescence and early adult life.

Cognitive deficits are a fundamental aspect of the disability of autism.

Does autism change over time?

Yes, autism does change over time.

Stone (1997) described the classic picture of autism in a young pre-school aged child as one who exhibits a marked lack of interest in others, failure in empathy, and absent or severely delayed speech and communication.

Marked resistance to change, restricted interests and stereotyped movements may develop or become more noticeable after three years of age.

The form and degree of features may change markedly as the child grows older but the core social, communication and behavioural difficulties persist. Many parents find the pre-school years most difficult to manage but, with early intervention and education, improvement can be expected.

With education and training primary school aged children usually become more socially responsive and communication skills increase. Self-stimulatory behaviours, problems in coping with change and transitions and disruptive or compulsive behaviour may increase at this time.

Adolescence can also bring the development of symptoms such as aggressive and oppositional or obsessive compulsive behaviour, and an increase in anxiety, tension and mood disturbance. Depressive illness is not uncommon and is probably due to a combination of the development of some degree of insight as well as hormonal and central nervous system (CNS) functional changes (Prior and Tonge 1990; Wing 1988).

There is a relatively increased risk for the development of seizures in adolescence. Estimates indicate that 25 per cent to 40 per cent of people with autism develop epilepsy before the age of 30. Gillberg and Steffenburg (1987) noted an increased risk for boys.

WHAT IS THE LONG-TERM OUTCOME?

Outcome, or follow-up, studies of people with autism in later life are few. Venter, Lord and Schopler (1992) studied higher-functioning adolescents and adults to determine the role of cognitive and behavioural factors in predicting later social-adaptive and academic achievement. They found that early verbal skills were the best predictor of both academic functioning and adaptive behaviour later in life. Gillberg and Steffenburg (1987) followed 46 cases into early adulthood and found that 60 per cent to 75 per cent had relatively poor outcomes in social adjustment. Of these about half were institutionalized.

During adulthood the majority of persons with autism are likely to require some level of support. For example, one study found that two thirds of the group were in day or residential treatment programmes (Goode, Rutter and Howlin 1994). A minority are able to work and live independently and have some social contact and friendships. Another minority deteriorate or need high levels of care.

In a recent study Howlin *et al.* (2004) reported on the adult outcome of 68 individuals with autism who in childhood had a performance IQ over 50. At follow-up their average age was 29 years. Overall, the majority had poor outcome with only 22 per cent having a 'very good' or 'good' outcome and most remained dependent on support services. Few lived alone or had permanent employment, communication remained impaired, reading and spelling abilities were poor and ten had developed epilepsy.

It is usually those adults who have higher levels of cognitive and communication skills that are able to live independently and remain in employment; however, some difficulties with social interaction remain. The majority of people with autism will experience behavioural, emotional and social problems throughout life, but nevertheless will make some developmental improvement and progressively become more independent.

Unfortunately in the young child with autism there is no way of knowing with confidence what the developmental trajectory will bring.

Do young people with autism have additional emotional and behavioural problems?

Children and adolescents with autism may have high levels of anxiety and mood disturbance and disruptive and self-absorbed behaviour, as well as communication disturbance and social relating problems.

The high levels of emotional and behavioural disturbance often persist throughout childhood and adolescence.

ANTI-SOCIAL BEHAVIOUR

Anti-social behaviours that require social intention and awareness, such as lying, stealing, hiding, lighting fires and refusing to go to school or work, are seldom seen in autism as they require a degree of social knowledge and skill beyond most young people with autism. However, behaviour perceived by others as anti-social may occur in persons with autism, particularly in those with higher intellectual abilities, as a manifestation of an obsessional preoccupation or self-stimulatory activity without social intent or understanding of the impact on others. For example, one young man regularly set fire to the hay shed on the family farm because he enjoyed the sight, sound and smell of the flames.

DISRUPTIVE BEHAVIOUR

Disruptive behaviour, such as tantrums, noisiness, abusiveness, impatience, aggression, self-injury and stubbornness, is problematic for clinicians, family and teachers alike.

In the school setting, disruptive behaviour has been found to relate directly to a loss of productive learning time. Disruptive behaviours are also likely to contribute to failure of integrated school placement in a mainstream setting and the rise of more restricted special school placements. High levels of disruptive behaviour also contribute to parental burden and are the main reason for placement of children into respite care or residential care.

ANXIETY

Young people with autism often have high levels of anxiety. The symptoms of anxious behaviour include fear of separation from familiar people, specific fears or phobias (e.g. certain sounds, smells, objects, animals), resistance to change (e.g. new clothes, food, routines), panic and emotional distress for little or no apparent reason, tenseness, shyness and irritability. These co-morbid symptoms of anxiety, apart from the distress they cause the child, have the potential to disrupt education, further impair social interaction and create management problems and stress for the parents and carers.

The identification of anxiety in a child with autism creates an opportunity for management. Psychological treatments, particularly cognitive and behavioural approaches, are effective treatments. Pharmacological treatments, such as selective serotonin re-uptake inhibitors and tri-cyclic anti-depressants, may also reduce anxiety in children. Psychological treatments might need some modification in order to compensate for language impairment, and the effectiveness of pharmacological treatments need to be confirmed using baseline and follow-up records of target symptoms.

These co-morbid emotional and behavioural problems are not confined to young children with autism, but remain a challenge for parents and carers at least into adolescence. Further follow-up studies are required to follow the changes in psychopathology into adult life.

DEPRESSION

Adolescents with autism are at increased risk of suffering depression and mood disturbance with associated symptoms of irritability, sleep and appetite disturbance (inducing weight loss), obsessional thoughts and preoccupations, compulsive behaviours, psychomotor retardation, and thoughts of suicide with a potential to act on these thoughts. These symptoms of mood disorder are likely to impair their education and school adjustment, further handicap their already compromised social interactions and interfere with the quality of their family life.

Depression responds to psychological treatments such as cognitive therapy, relaxation training and pleasant events scheduling modified according to the intellectual ability of the young person. Rewarding experience, reduction of stress at home and school and attention to parental mental health are helpful. Anti-depressant medication may also be necessary if the depression is severe or persistent.

ATTENTION DEFICIT HYPERACTIVITY

Distractibility, lack of concentration, impulsiveness, poor planning ability, disorganized behaviour, fidgetiness and motor overactivity are common symptoms in young people with autism but generally decrease with maturity. Management requires a broad approach including planned, structured, time-limited activities in simple steps, limitation of the amount of environmental stimulation, planning for change, communication programmes (e.g. visual systems), behaviour modification, relaxation and perhaps medication.

Approaches to treatment

There is no cure for autism. Many treatment approaches and therapies have been reported during the past four decades often without strong empirical evidence of benefit. Many of these were based on specific theories of causation. Some came and went quickly, such as swimming with dolphins, whilst others became outdated (e.g. aversive therapies) as knowledge increased and social approaches to disability and ethics changed.

Current treatment usually consists of well-designed, multidisciplinary structured treatment programmes that incorporate developmental approaches with early intervention, special education, behavioural management, social and communication skills training and medication when indicated. Treatment must be a collaborative approach between the family/carers and the professionals involved in the child's care. In 2001, the USA National Academy of Science (NRC 2001) concluded that no single approach has been found to be best for all people with autism. Treatment approaches will probably differ across time for an individual with autism.

BEHAVIOURAL APPROACHES

Behavioural approaches to the education, treatment and management of young people with autism have been successfully used for the past three decades. It is now clear that behaviour management techniques lead to a reduction in difficult behaviour and may increase social, communicative and cognitive skills in some people with autism.

Traditional approaches

In traditional behaviour management, the target behavioural problem is studied, then the environment is manipulated in such a way as to increase, decrease or maintain the behaviour. This is referred to as the ABC approach. The target Behaviour to be managed is described and then either the Antecedents and/or the Consequences of the behaviour are manipulated. For persons with autism, the treatment programme comprises a set of procedures designed to reduce behavioural excesses (e.g. self-stimulation, obsessions, self-injurious behaviour) and to increase behavioural competence (e.g. attention to task, language and social skills). Current behaviour management combines the teaching of new skills together with the suppression of undesirable behaviours. There are several ways of encouraging and increasing new behaviours.

POSITIVE REINFORCEMENT

This is the easiest and most often used method of strengthening behaviour. By following the target behaviour with a pleasant event we are increasing the likelihood of that behaviour occurring again. One of the trickiest things here is to work out what the child actually finds pleasant. We must not assume that what we find pleasant and rewarding will be shared by others, particularly children with autism. For example, we may find attention in the form of a hug and a kiss very pleasant, but for the child with autism this may actually be experienced as unpleasant and overwhelming.

TIME-OUT

This strategy is widely known and used to decrease undesirable behaviours in young children. The underlying principle is that most people like to be rewarded with attention or some other positive feedback when a behaviour has occurred. If that behaviour is met with no positive reinforcement, and the child is actually removed from any opportunity of attention, the behaviour is less likely to happen again. The child may be taken to another room or merely sent to another part of the room he/she is currently in and ignored for a short time. This method does rely on the child being able to link the two events, recognizing that he/she is receiving no attention because of what he/she has just done. For some children with autism, the removal to a quiet and empty space may actually be rewarding and lead to an increase in some behaviour in order to achieve isolation.

Time-out can be effective as a 'circuit breaker' for both child and parent when a break or separation is needed to stop a situation from escalating. Time-out for the parent and child to cool down, and the parent to think through how best to respond. Time-out is best used in conjunction with methods that teach new or replacement behaviours.

PROMPTING

This is a procedure that is used when the required behaviour does not exist at all. The child is guided to perform the response. There are a number of ways to prompt a child.

Physical prompts are literally 'hands on' attempts to encourage the new behaviour. For example, if the new behaviour required is for the child to eat using a fork rather than his fingers, the physical prompt will involve putting your hand over the child's on the fork and helping him to stab the food and lift it to his mouth.

Verbal prompts involve telling the child what to do. For example, 'Stab your food with the fork.' Verbal prompts need to be very explicit and concrete at first. It is not sufficient just to say 'Use your fork' as it does not tell the child exactly what he should be using the fork for (e.g. he may decide to 'use his fork' to poke the cat).

Pointing can also be used to prompt the correct response. Eventually the prompt will fade and become unnecessary over time. At first a combination of prompts is usually required. For example, a physical prompt will be combined with a verbal prompt that clearly tells the child what to do as he is doing it. As the behaviour is improving, the physical prompt may be dropped and a point and verbal prompt used instead.

Subtle prompts can be used very successfully with older children where a new behaviour has been learnt but the child still needs just a little cue or reminder of what to do. For example, in the classroom, a child who continually shouted out to contribute enthusiastically to the class had to learn to put up his hand and wait for the teacher to say his name. The cue he continued to need was simply the teacher raising a finger to indicate that he needed to raise his hand. The benefit of a small cue is that it helps the child without being obvious to everyone else.

SHAPING

This method involves encouraging and reinforcing successive approximations of the new behaviour until the behaviour is learnt. For example, if the child is unable to wave goodbye, any attempt to raise a hand or arm in response to your waving goodbye is rewarded. It may begin with only a slight movement. As the child gets better at raising her arm and moving her hand you wait until both occur before giving the reinforcer. The child learns that more is expected of her in gradual steps until the whole wave is learnt.

Shaping is a useful method to use with young children at any developmental level. It does not require the child to have an existing level of speech or comprehension of speech. Shaping can be used without spoken instructions, although praise and encouragement through words usually accompany the reinforcer. It does require some ability in the child to attend and imitate an action.

CHAINING

This is a useful way of teaching a more complex behaviour or task and involves breaking it down into small steps. The steps are then taught one at a time. As each step is learnt, the next is taught. You cannot miss steps, or teach them out of logical order.

Self-help skills such as dressing are often taught using this method – for example, pulling up pants. The task has a lot of different steps which need to be thought about and written down. If you are forward chaining, you start with the first step which may be picking the pants up in both hands. The next step may then be lifting one leg to step into the pants etc. If you are using backward chaining you teach the other way around and start with the last step which would be the final pulling up of the pants.

Chaining breaks down the task into tiny steps that do not overwhelm the child and you work through one step at a time until the whole task has been learnt. Success builds on success as each step is mastered. This method is very successful when teaching young children with few skills and little language.

Understanding the communicative function of difficult behaviour

More recent approaches try to understand the *function* or *purpose* of particular behaviour and what the person is trying to tell us; that is, the *communicative function* of the behaviour. Current behaviour management programmes for persons with autism take into account more than the ABC approach, considering individual variables, environmental factors and how the ability to communicate is affecting behaviour. For example, disruptive behaviours such as aggression, self-injury and stereotypies may have many communicative functions such as:

- to get help or attention
- to escape from stressful situations or activities
- to obtain desired objects
- to protest against unwanted events/activities
- to obtain stimulation.

If the communicative function of the behaviour can be determined, then it is possible to teach a substitute behaviour that helps the person to get his/her message across more appropriately.

EARLY INTERVENTION

There have been numerous approaches to early intervention for children with autism. These include: home-based versus school-based programmes; integrated versus specialist autism settings; length of intervention varying from 4 to 40-plus hours per week. Most treatments report gains in symbolic play, language and social interaction. Early intervention programmes employ both behavioural and special education techniques. Professional teaching support is vital for those family members and carers who are working on treatment programmes at home as they are generally intensive and demanding.

Claims that highly intensive behaviourally based interventions lead to recovery or normal functioning are controversial. Behavioural interventions probably lead to improvements, particularly in scores on IQ tests; however, suggestions that initial benefits are maintained over time require replication. Lovaas, Calouri and Jada (1989) proposed that Applied Behaviour Analysis (ABA), an intensive intervention (40-plus hours per week, for two years or more), led to recovery from autism in a small sample of children. Replicating this early intervention in order to study its effectiveness has been difficult, particularly sustaining the 40 hours per week of training, and no study to date has been able to do that. Despite this, many parents report high satisfaction with ABA programmes. Longer-term evaluations of intensive programmes are needed, particularly those that measure social communication and interaction, conceptual abilities, obsessional and ritualistic behaviours, and the additional emotional and behavioural problems associated with autism.

The specific effects of early intervention require further study, particularly the effects of different treatments and the responses of sub-groups of children with autism, such as lower and higher-functioning children.

TEACHING AND SPECIAL EDUCATION

Special educational programmes for children with autism are individually designed by teachers using a problem solving approach to address specific needs. These programmes aim to provide predictable, consistent and highly organized teaching situations in the classroom. The child's specific cognitive profile needs to be considered, for example the use of visual-based rather than verbal instruction will improve outcome in the child with good visual-motor skills. The response to teaching is related to the severity of intellectual and language impairment; however, most children make some gains when behavioural methods and special educational approaches are used.

The move to integrate children with autism into as normal a learning situation as possible is generally appropriate. Placement in mainstream or special education schools is generally dependent upon the child's intellectual level. Integration is a desirable principle; however, some children with autism have difficulty without close supervision and support. Without adequate special resources and teaching, children with autism are at risk of becoming more isolated and unoccupied, or may become more disruptive and disturbed.

COMMUNICATION SKILLS PROGRAMMES

It is not possible to put appropriate intervention programmes (either language or behavioural) in place without careful assessment of the person's current level of cognitive and language functioning. Lower-functioning or non-verbal people with autism also require assessment of possible communicative intent in their behaviour (e.g. the child who hits himself when he wants an activity to stop). For those who have speech, it is also important to assess pragmatic (the social use of speech) abilities. Recently, more attention has been paid to the effects of communication problems on behaviour in order to replace inappropriate behaviour with more effective communication, for example using a picture system.

Augmentative communication helps those who are non-verbal to communicate by using other systems. These systems are called 'augmentative' because they augment or increase the strength of the person's power to communicate. Visual systems using simple pictures and line drawings, signing systems and also photographs are often used to augment communication for children with autism. Each person must be carefully assessed to determine which system will suit him/her best. The choice of system to help improve communication will depend upon level of cognitive and language ability. Three systems frequently used are signing, the COMPIC (computer generated pictures) system, and also photographs and objects.

Signing was probably the first alternative system used with non-verbal children with autism. At first, the signing systems used by the deaf were taught, but these are complex systems that require finger spelling of words and use abstract concepts. In the early 1980s, a simpler system called Makaton was devised to use with children with intellectual disability. This system has varying degrees of difficulty, but at its easiest level signs learnt are simple, concrete and do not require difficult finger spelling. Many of the first signs learnt use only one hand. For example, the sign for drink uses one hand in the shape of a cup that is lifted to the mouth and tilted as if the child were having a drink.

One advantage of signs is that they are very portable and do not require the child to carry around equipment. Another advantage of establishing a signing system is that it has been found to encourage speech in children, rather than what many parents fear, that it would reduce the chance of their child talking. However, signing is not widely understood in the community and the child may not always be well understood outside the circle of those who can sign with him/her. Signing does also require that the child can attend to the person teaching the signs and also imitate an action.

COMPIC and *PECS* are used successfully in many teaching programmes. COMPICs are very simple and clear line drawings that represent a wide range of objects, actions, feelings etc. They can be used initially at a very simple, but practical, level with young children who learn to point at the picture or show the picture to indicate their needs. When children are familiar with a number of these pictures, they can be put into a wallet of pictures that the child carries with him/her and takes out to indicate his/her needs. The child gradually builds up a vocabulary of pictures to meet his/her own special needs. COMPIC programmes are widely available in computer software format and loose-leaf book. COMPIC pictures are easily understood by everyone and do not require the child to learn and remember complex actions, as does signing. Children who have low cognitive skills can generally use a picture system in a simple way to communicate more effectively.

The Picture Exchange Communication System (PECS) (Frost and Bondy 1994) is another augmentative communication system. Developed in the early 1990s, PECS is widely used in early intervention and school programmes to teach children how to initiate communication. An advantage of this system is that it does not require complex or expensive materials and can be used in a variety of settings by parents, carers and teachers. PECS begins with teaching a student to exchange a picture of a desired item with a teacher who immediately honours the request. Verbal prompts are not used.

Once this step is mastered, the system goes on to teach discrimination of symbols and later simple 'sentences' are made from stringing together these symbols. Children can also learn to comment and answer direct questions using symbols as in the COMPIC system.

Photographs of objects and people in the child's world can be used effectively with lower-functioning children who cannot master the use of symbols or line drawings. Use of photographs usually requires that the child first learns to match an object with a photograph of that object. The child learns that the photograph represents the object. The photograph must be simple, clear and uncluttered. After the child has learnt to match photographs and objects, the more complex concept of matching photograph and activity or action can be taught.

Once the child is able to recognize a number of photographs, a photo vocabulary can be built up in the same way as a COMPIC vocabulary. Photographs can be used to help the child understand timetables or the steps involved in completing an activity. For example, the classroom may have photographs of the day's activities pinned to the wall. When each activity finishes, the child may put away that photograph. Similarly, when the child is required to get dressed, the steps involved may be pinned to his/her bedroom door in the correct sequence and easily followed.

Objects can be used in a similar way to photographs with children who have difficulty understanding photographs. Object timetables are useful. Objects that represent activities can be laid out or stuck on the wall to show the child what happens next. For example, a crayon means work at the table, and the next object is a juice box straw to represent that snack time comes after work. A great advantage of photographs and objects is that the child can attend to them for as long as he/she needs to, and also return to them to refresh his/her memory. This is not possible with a sign where once the sign has been demonstrated, it is gone.

SOCIAL SKILLS PROGRAMMES

Social impairment in autism affects most aspects of the person's functioning. The approaches used to treat social difficulties vary according to the needs of each person with autism, particularly their level of cognitive ability, age and the nature of their social impairment. For example, the young child with autism who is aloof and withdraws from social contact requires a very different programme to an older, more able adolescent who attempts to join in with others but shows little empathy or reciprocity. Areas covered may include social isolation, understanding about friends and strangers, social play skills, interacting with peers, understanding rules and when they may be broken, understanding emotions and increasing imaginative and social imitative play. Treatment for young children with autism initially involves the teaching of social skills according to specific, inflexible rules that can be learnt in specific situations, such as 'Do not touch other people's knees when you are on the bus'. As children grow older social skills training may include the use of:

- *Picture scripts* (drawings that represent social situations and how to handle them): to rehearse social situations and teach a range of appropriate responses.

- *Social stories*: to help understand social situations, routines and make judgements about a social situation on an individual basis. Details are gathered about a problem situation (the target), the person's abilities, interests and responses, and others involved. These details are used to form a story. The person is given information about the situation and how to respond. Stories can be written, or presented as videotapes or audio tapes for those who cannot read.

- *Social skills groups*: including the involvement of competent peers can be helpful to teach social interaction skills. Role-play activities and use of videotapes are helpful in teaching and practising social interaction skills and enable the person with autism to observe his/her behaviour and practise correct responses.

PHARMACOTHERAPY

There is no drug available that will cure autism. There is empirical evidence of variable quality regarding the effectiveness of drugs in the treatment of various behaviours, symptoms and psychopathological disorders associated with autism.

The use of medication should only occur as part of a comprehensive management plan that includes approaches to improving communication, behaviour management, education, social skills training, structuring of daily routine, and parent support.

Drugs should only be presented after assessment and diagnosis have defined the symptoms or disorder. To some extent the use of any treatment is experimental, therefore when using drugs it is necessary to record baseline and follow-up descriptions of the target symptoms, for example using a behaviour checklist in order to demonstrate change. Baseline assessment of abnormal movements helps distinguish these from any later drug-induced movements. Regular inquiry regarding possible side effects is also necessary. Compliance with treatment is improved when the family or carers and the person with autism are involved in regular review of management.

Anxiety

- Tricyclic anti-depressants (TCAs) (e.g. Imipramine), but not when there is a history of heart disease, due to potential cardiotoxic effects, or epilepsy.

- Selective serotonin re-uptake inhibitors (SSRIs) (e.g. Fluoxetine, Paroxetine, Sertraline). Excitation, disinhibition, nausea and headache may be troublesome side effects.

- Neuroleptics (e.g. Haloperidol, Risperidone, Phenothiazines) in low dose as a last resort due to potential neurological side effects (dystonia, akathisia, dyskinesias), weight gain and, rarely, blood disorders.

- Buspirone – some limited evidence.

Depression

- SSRIs.

- TCAs for older adolescents.

Obsessive compulsive symptoms

- SSRIs.

- TCAs, particularly Clomipramine and Imipramine, but these may unmask epilepsy.

Frustration, rage, aggression, disruptive behaviour and withdrawal

- Neuroleptics (Haloperidol is the drug of choice).

- Naltrexone – may reduce self-injurious behaviour and hyperactivity. Monitor liver function.

- Anti-convulsants (e.g. Valproate, Carbamazepine) may improve learning. Monitor liver function.

Cyclic mood disorder

- Lithium – requires regular serum level and renal function monitoring. Avoid dehydration. May also reduce self-injurious behaviour and aggression.

- Anti-convulsants (as above).

Attention deficit hyperactivity symptoms

- Stimulants (e.g. Dexamphetamine). Symptoms need to be unequivocal. Frequent side effects (mood disturbance, irritability, worsening hyperactivity, withdrawal and stereotypies, insomnia and tics) limit usefulness.

- Neuroleptics.

- TCAs (see above).

- Buspirone.

- Naltrexone.

Are there any guidelines to help choose a specific treatment?

Given our current state of knowledge, there is not necessarily only one way to manage a child with autism. There may be a variety of different ways of approaching management.

A multi-modal approach to treatment is more likely to promote development, improve behaviour and reduce stress experienced by the child and family.

Freeman (1997) recommended asking the following questions before choosing a specific treatment:

- Will the treatment result in harm to the child (physical or psychological harm)?

- Is the treatment developmentally appropriate for the child?

- How will failure of the treatment affect my child and family?

- Has the treatment been validated scientifically?

- How will the treatment be integrated into the child's current programme?

SOME POINTS TO REMEMBER ABOUT TREATMENT

- Beware of treatments that promise 'cure'.

- Beware of treatments that are said to work for *all* children with autism.

- Detailed assessments and behaviour, language, cognitive and social skills baselines must be completed before any treatment programme can begin so that change can be documented and measured.

- Intervention must be sensitive to the development level and skills of each child with autism if it is to be effective. For example, the use of signing is not indicated if the child is unable to imitate or follow visual cues.

- 'Do not become so infatuated with a given treatment that functional curriculum, vocational life and social skills are ignored' (Freeman 1997, p.649).

Treatment studies remain a priority for research. These are however difficult to conduct and fund. The efficacy of behavioural and educational interventions and the cost effectiveness of such programmes often lack solid data. Volkmar *et al.* (2004) recently concluded: 'A major concern is the large, and possibly growing, gap between what science can show is effective, on the one hand, and what treatments parents actually pursue' (p.155).

Asperger's disorder

What is Asperger's disorder?

One year after Kanner's original paper on autism, Hans Asperger published a paper in 1944 that described what was to become known as Asperger's disorder. Both Kanner and Asperger trained in medicine in Vienna but, unlike Kanner, who moved to the US, Asperger remained working in Europe.

Asperger and Kanner were apparently unaware of each other's work, probably because of World War II. Asperger's paper remained relatively unknown as it was published in German and was not widely available in translation.

Asperger's paper described a group of children and adolescents who had deficits in communication and social skills, had obsessional interests and behaviour, disliked change and had a dependence on rituals and routines. In addition many were physically clumsy.

Unlike the children described by Kanner, the children in Asperger's paper generally had no significant delays in early cognitive or language development. Asperger described this condition as *autistic psychopathy*.

There has been increasing interest in Hans Asperger and his syndrome over the past 20 years. In the early 1990s, Asperger's paper was translated by Frith (1991) and became more widely available. Since that time Asperger's disorder has been more frequently used to describe a group of children who presented with developmental deficits in social skills and behaviour but were difficult to classify.

For the past decade or so there has been a continuing debate as to whether or not Asperger's disorder is a type of autism or whether it constitutes a separate disorder. Many publications have tried to delineate the boundaries, if any, between autism and Asperger's disorder.

Despite the differences that can be seen when looking at the original cases described by both Kanner and Asperger, there is continuing confusion over the diagnostic criteria for Asperger's disorder, particularly as subsequent accounts and case studies have not necessarily adhered to the criteria suggested by Asperger himself. The principal areas of inconsistency relate to early development in the areas of cognition, motor skills and language.

The DSM-IV and the ICD-10 have attempted to introduce a consistent international approach to diagnosis and specify that the key differentiation is that persons with Asperger's disorder do not have delayed language development which is a characteristic of autistic disorder. Persons with Asperger's disorder have overall normal intellectual ability. Approximately 20 per cent of persons with autistic disorder also have IQ in the normal range and are referred to as high-functioning.

How common is Asperger's disorder?

Asperger's disorder was thought to be more common than autism. Ehlers and Gillberg (1993) studied a population of Swedish children and suggested an incidence of 36 per 10,000 compared with an incidence of about 10 per 10,000 for autism. Because of the lack of diagnostic clarity, estimates of prevalence should be treated circumspectly. It is very likely that mild degrees of Asperger's disorder may not cause sufficient social, emotional or mental health problems for recognition to be necessary or even desirable, except perhaps for epidemiological purposes. One of the most reliable current estimates of the prevalence of people with Asperger's disorder who have needs for a service is that of Fombonne (2003), who concluded that 2.5 in 10,000 of the general population met accepted criteria for the disorder.

Some small-scale epidemiological studies suggest that the ratio of males to females is about 10:1. Both prevalence and gender distribution figures require confirmation by larger-scale epidemiological studies, and at this stage are only rough estimates.

Age of onset

Asperger's disorder tends to be diagnosed later than autism in young children. Neither ICD-10 nor DSM-IV stipulates the criteria for age of onset as they do for autism. However, in his original paper, Asperger described children as having difficulties by the age of two.

Parents of young children with autism often recognize problems with behaviour and, in particular, language development by about 18 months to two years of age. Because children with Asperger's disorder do not have delayed early language, or problems with cognitive development, there are few early signs that all is not well. It is more usual for parents to become concerned about their child's emerging unusual or odd behaviour and social development but these tend to be identified later, usually from about three to four years of age.

Diagnosis of Asperger's disorder may not occur until the child has attended pre-school or some other early childhood setting such as crèche. This is probably because the child's social and behavioural problems become more noticeable when the child is seen with peers in a more structured social setting where there are more demands for social interaction.

Diagnosis

In the interest of avoiding confusion for the person, his/her family, clinicians and re-searchers it is advocated that the DSM-IV/ICD-10 criteria should be applied. One practical answer to the lack of clarity about diagnosis is to break diagnosis down into three steps:

1.   Does a person have a pervasive developmental disorder?
2.   Is there a history of delayed language development?
3.   Is the person of overall normal intellectual ability; that is, is he or she high-functioning?

This approach has some advantages. It may be more reliable to diagnose the presence of a pervasive developmental disorder than to make a diagnosis of a specific pervasive developmental disorder. Many professionals use Wing and Gould's triad of social impairments (see Box 1) as a guide to the presence of a pervasive developmental disorder and indeed elements of the triad are apparent in both the ICD-10 and the DSM-IV criteria.

Box 1: The triad of social impairments (adapted from Wing and Gould 1979)

Absence or impairment of:
1.   comprehension and use of communication, both verbal and non-verbal
2.   two-way social interaction
3.   true, flexible, imaginative activities, with the substitution of a narrow range of repetitive, stereotyped pursuits.

Another advantage of this pragmatic approach is that it is needs based. More able people with either high-functioning autism or Asperger's disorder do need very different services than less able people. They are much more self-reflective and are therefore very conscious of their environment. More able adolescents and adults with hig- functioning autism or Asperger's disorder may have been sensitized to humiliation and may have consequently become very sensitive to status. They may therefore be very intolerant of receiving help in a mixed group containing people who are much more handicapped than themselves. Finally, more able people with autism or Asperger's disorder may be capable of considerable or even complete independence and autonomy, and the services that they receive should reflect this.

The presentation and skills of a person with a pervasive developmental disorder may change over time and a less able child may grow into a more able adult. Children with autism and normal intellectual ability will probably develop into adults with adequate language ability, although they are still likely to have problems with the social and conversational use of language. In these cases, the diagnosis of high functioning autism would continue to apply. Although adults diagnosed with high functioning autism and those with Asperger's disorder are likely to have a number of features in common, their differing developmental pathways, particularly with respect to language development, produce neuro-cognitive and behavioural differences.

The adjustment of a person with a pervasive developmental disorder is the end result of the interaction of various neuro-cognitive disabilities, a person's way of coping with them, and the impact of other people's reactions to them. Applying this 'functional' diagnostic approach leads to a multilevel assessment (see Box 2). The profile of specific disabilities so obtained will distinguish Asperger's disorder from autistic disorder, but it will also be found that each person will differ slightly and each will therefore have their own personality and profile of strengths and weaknesses.

Box 2: Multilevel approach to assessment

Level 1. Examine the patient, obtain systematic developmental information. What developmental disorders are present?

Level 2. Talk to the patient and a key informant. How have the patient's developmental difficulties been affected by their emotional reactions to them? How have they been influenced by other factors, such as age, intelligence, anxiety levels and co-morbidity?

Level 3. Talk to the patient, talk to a family member, consider other professional reports. How has the patient's reactions to their disabilities been influenced by other people's reactions to them? Has the patient been victimized? What have been the family's expectations of, and reactions to, the patient?

What causes Asperger's disorder?

There is widespread agreement that genetic factors predominate as the primary cause of Asperger's disorder. Asperger himself noted that, in all cases where he studied the family closely, similar traits were found to some degree in parents and other family members. Later studies have found similar autistic traits in the relatives of young people with Asperger's disorder.

Children and young people with Asperger's disorder

Some examples of how Asperger's disorder affects children:

- Acquisition of language follows a normal or even accelerated pattern, but content of speech is abnormal – pedantic – and may centre on one or two favoured topics.

- Little facial expression, vocal intonation may be monotonous and tone may be inappropriate.

- Impairment in two-way social interaction including an inability to understand the rules governing social behaviour. May be easily led.

- Problems with social comprehension despite superior verbal skills.

- Very rigid, prefers structure.

- Well developed verbal memory skills, absorb facts easily, generally good level of performance at maths and science.

- Highly anxious with a dislike of any form of criticism or imperfection.

- Most attend mainstream schools and are often victims of teasing which causes withdrawal into isolated activities.

- Are seen to be 'odd' or 'eccentric'.

Are there any differences between autism and Asperger's disorder?

The simple answer to this question is yes. The recent debate as to whether or not the two disorders differ is clouded because clinicians have not used a consistent set of diagnostic criteria to characterize their subject populations when exploring the differences between Asperger's disorder and autism. This variability of diagnostic assignment has led to a situation where studies examining the validity of Asperger's disorder as a separate disorder, particularly in contrast to high-functioning autism, cannot be easily compared, or interpreted. This problem can be addressed by the use of the ICD-10 and DSM-IV definitions and diagnostic criteria.

For example, a recent study (Tonge *et al.* 1999) of high-functioning autism and Asperger's disorder strictly defined by DSM-IV criteria found that children and adolescents with Asperger's disorder presented with higher levels of overall psychopathology, were more disruptive, anti-social and anxious, and had more problems with social relationships than the children with high-functioning autism. These differences were not due to any age or global IQ differences.

The finding of high levels of anxiety and disruptive behaviour in the Asperger's group has particular clinical relevance as these psychopathological problems are potentially open to treatment. Anxiety symptoms may be responsive to cognitive behavioural interventions and psychopharmacological treatment. Disruptive behaviours can be modified by educational, environmental and behavioural modification techniques.

In the absence of identifiable neurological damage, neurobehavioural studies have indicated differences between autism and Asperger's disorder. While there are broad similarities in the clinical (e.g. social dysfunction) and neuropsychological (e.g. visual-perceptual processing anomalies) features associated with high-functioning autism and Asperger's disorder, recent research has identified differences in executive functioning, lateralization and motor ability, supporting the notion of a differing neurobiological basis. For example, a recent series of experiments have indicated that executive functioning, in particular inhibitory deficiencies, is quantitatively and qualitatively different in autism and Asperger's disorder (Rinehart *et al.* 2001b). Individuals with autism had difficulty inhibiting cognitive-motor responses at increasing levels of task complexity. In contrast, individuals with Asperger's disorder performed similarly to age and IQ matched controls. It was noted that a combination of inhibitory and set-shifting deficits may have accounted for performance deterioration in the autism group. Interestingly, past researchers have emphasized only set-shifting, but not inhibitory, deficiencies in autism (Ozonoff and Jensen 1999). Further, young people with autism are significantly slower at shifting attention from local to global features of a numerical configuration than those with Asperger's disorder who had no such difficulty (Rinehart *et al.* 2001b).

MOTOR FUNCTIONING

Clinical observation suggested that motor clumsiness is a feature which might distinguish Asperger's disorder from autism (Tantam 1988). In reviewing the literature, Ghaziuddin, Tsai and Ghaziuddin (1992) found that approximately 50 per cent of publications referred to clumsy, uncoordinated movement patterns in either single case studies or group studies of children with Asperger's disorder. Gillberg (1989) observed that individuals with Asperger's disorder 'appeared to be generally clumsy', had a 'stiff or awkward way of walking (often without arm-swing)' and were 'uncoordinated in posture and gesture' (p.528). Recent functional magnetic resonance imaging data has revealed that individuals with autism exhibit less pronounced activation in the primary motor cortex and supplementary-motor-area during a simple finger tapping task than individuals with Asperger's disorder who do not exhibit a decrease in supplementary-motor-area activity but show a prolonged activation following the movement (Muller *et al.* 2001; Rinehart *et al.* 2001a). If the mechanism for terminating motor movement before another is initiated is dysfunctional in Asperger's disorder, this could account for their clumsiness.

References

American Psychiatric Association (1994) *Diagnostic and Statistical Manual of Mental Disorders (fourth edition)*. Washington, DC: American Psychiatric Association Press.

Asperger, H. (1944) 'Die "Autistichen Psychopathen" in Kindersalter.' *Archiv fur Psychiatrie und Nervenkrankenheiten 117*, 76–136.

Bailey, A., Phillips, W. and Rutter, M. (1996) 'Autism: towards an integration of clinical, genetic, neuropsychological, and neurobiological perspectives.' *Journal of Child Psychology and Psychiatry 37*, 89–126.

Baron-Cohen, S., Allen, J. and Gillberg, C. (1992) 'Can autism be detected at 18 months? The needle, and the CHAT.' *British Journal of Psychiatry 161*, 839–934.

Berument, S., Rutter, M., Lord, C., Pickles, A. and Bailey, A. (1999) 'Autism screening questionnaire: diagnostic validity.' *British Journal of Psychiatry 175*, 444–451.

Bettelheim, B. (1967) *The Empty Fortress*. New York: The Free Press.

COMPIC (1992) *Your Guide to COMPIC*. Melbourne, Australia: Spastic Society of Victoria.

Ehlers, S. and Gillberg, C. (1993) 'The epidemiology of Asperger's disorder: a total population study.' *Journal of Psychology and Psychiatry and Allied Disciplines 34*, 1327–1350.

Einfeld, S.L. and Tonge, B.J. (1992) *Manual for the Developmental Behaviour Checklist.* Clayton, Melbourne and Sydney: Monash University Centre for Developmental Psychiatry and School of Psychiatry, University of N.S.W.

Folstein, S. and Rutter, M. (1977) 'Infantile autism: a genetic case study of 21 twin pairs.' *Journal of Child Psychology and Psychiatry 18*, 297–321.

Fombonne, E. (2003) 'Epidemiological surveys of autism and other pervasive developmental disorders.' *Journal of Autism and Developmental Disorders 33*, 365–382.

Freeman, B. (1997) 'Guidelines for evaluating intervention programs for children with autism.' *Journal of Autism and Developmental Disorders 27*, 641–651.

Frith, U. (ed) (1991) *Autism and Asperger Syndrome*. Cambridge: Cambridge University Press.

Frost, L. and Bondy, A. (1994) *The Picture Exchange Communication System: Training Manual.* Newark, DE: Pyramid Educational Consultants, Inc.

Ghaziuddin, M., Tsai, L. and Ghaziuddin, N. (1992) 'Brief report: a comparison of the diagnostic criteria for Asperger Syndrome.' Special Issue on Classification and Diagnosis. *Journal of Autism and Developmental Disorders 22*, 643–649.

Gillberg, C. (1989) 'Asperger's disorder in 23 Swedish children.' *Developmental Medicine and Child Neurology 31*, 520–531.

Gillberg, C. and Steffenburg, S. (1987) 'Outcome and prognostic factors in infantile autism and similar conditions: a population-based study of 46 cases followed through puberty.' *Journal of Autism and Developmental Disorders 17*, 273–287.

REFERENCES

Goode, S., Rutter, M. and Howlin, P. (1994) *A Twenty-Year Follow-Up of Children with Autism.* Paper presented at the 13th Biennial Meeting of the International Society for the Study of Behavioural Development, Amsterdam, The Netherlands.

Gray, C. (1996) *Higher Functioning Adolescents and Young Adults with Autism.* Austin, TX: Pro-Ed.

Harris, S. (1994) 'Treatment of family problems in autism.' In E. Schopler and G. Mesibov (eds) *Behavioral Issues in Autism.* New York: Plenum Press.

Howlin, P. (1998) *Children with Autism and Asperger's Disorder: A Guide for Practitioners and Carers.* Chichester: John Wiley and Sons.

Howlin, P., Goode, S., Hutton, J. and Rutter, M. (2004) 'Adult outcome for children with autism.' *Journal of Child Psychology and Psychiatry 45*, 212–229.

Kanner, L. (1943) 'Autistic disturbances of affective contact.' *Nervous Child 2*, 217–250.

Koegel, R.L., Bimbela, A. and Schreibman, L. (1996) 'Collateral effects of family training on family interactions.' *Journal of Autism and Developmental Disorders 26*, 347–360.

Krug, D.A., Arick, J. and Almond, P. (1980) 'Behaviour checklist for identifying severely handicapped individuals with high levels of autistic behaviour.' *Journal of Child Psychology and Psychiatry 21*, 221–229.

Le Couteur, A., Rutter, M., Lord, C., Rios, P., Robertson, S., Holdgrafer, M. and McLennan, J. (1989) 'Autism diagnostic interview: a standardized investigator-based instrument.' *Journal of Autism and Developmental Disorders 19*, 363–387.

Lord, C., Rutter, M., Goode, S., Heemsbergen, J., Jordan, H., Mawhood, L. and Schopler, E. (1989) 'Autism diagnostic observation schedule: a standardized observation of communicative and social behaviour.' *Journal of Autism and Developmental Disorders 19*, 185–212.

Lovaas, I., Calouri, K. and Jada, J. (1989) 'The nature of behavioural treatment and research with young autistic persons.' In C. Gillberg (ed) *Diagnosis and Treatment of Autism.* New York: Plenum Press.

Lovejoy, D.W., Ball, J.D., Keats, M., Stutts, M.L., Spain, E.H., Janda, L. and Janusz, J. (1999) 'Neuropsychological performance of adults with attention deficit hyperactivity disorder (ADHD): diagnostic classification estimates for measures of frontal lobe/executive functioning.' *Journal of the International Neuropsychological Society 5*, 222–233.

Moes, M. and Frea, W. (2002) 'Cotextualised behavioural support in early intervention for children with autism and their families.' *Journal of Autism and Developmental Disorders 32*, 519–533.

Muller, R.A., Pierce, K., Ambrose, J.B., Allen, G. and Courchesne, E. (2001) 'Atypical patterns of cerebral motor activation in autism: a functional magnetic resonance study.' *Biological Psychology 49*, 665–676.

NRC (2001) *Educating Young Children with Autism.* Washington, DC: National Academy Press.

Ozonoff, S. and Jensen, J. (1999) 'Brief report: specific executive function profiles in three neurodevelopmental disorders.' *Journal of Autism and Developmental Disorders 29*, 171–177.

Prior, M. and Tonge, B.J. (1990) 'Pervasive developmental disorders.' In B.J. Tonge, G.D. Burrows and J. Werry (eds) *Handbook of Studies in Child Psychiatry* (Vol. 1). Amsterdam: Elsevier.

Quill, K.A. (2000) *Do–Watch–Listen–Say: Social Communication Intervention for Children with Autism.* Baltimore, MD: Paul H. Brookes.

Rinehart, N.J., Bradshaw, J.L., Brereton, A.V. and Tonge, B.J. (2001a) 'Movement preparation in high-functioning autism and Asperger's disorder: a serial choice-reaction time task involving motor reprogramming.' *Journal of Autism and Developmental Disorders 31*, 79–88.

Rinehart, N.J., Bradshaw, J.L., Moss, S., Brereton, A.V. and Tonge, B.J. (2001b) 'A deficit in shifting attention in high-functioning autism but not Asperger's disorder.' *Autism: Research and Practice 5*, 67–80.

Rutter, M. (1983) 'Cognitive deficits in the pathogenesis of autism.' *Journal of Child Psychology and Psychiatry 24*, 513–531.

Schopler, E., Reichler, R.J., Bashford, A., Lansing, M.D. and Marcus, L.M. (1990) *Individualized Assessment and Treatment for Autistic and Developmentally Disabled Children: Psychoeducational Profile–Revised (PEP-R).* Austin, TX: Pro-Ed.

Schopler, E., Reichler, R.J., DeVellis, R.F. and Daly, K. (1980) 'Toward objective classification of childhood autism: Childhood Autism Rating Scale (CARS).' *Journal of Autism and Developmental Disorders 10*, 91–103.

Schreibman, L. (1994) 'General principles of behaviour management.' E. Schopler and G. Mesibov (eds) *Behavioural Issues in Autism.* New York: Plenum Press.

Stone, W.L. (1997) 'Autism in infancy and early childhood.' In D.J. Cohen and F.R. Volkmar (eds) *Handbook of Autism and Pervasive Developmental Disorders (second edition).* New York: Wiley.

Tantam, D. (1988) 'Annotation: Asperger's syndrome.' *Journal of Child Psychology and Psychiatry 29*, 245–255.

Tidmarsh, L. and Volkmar, F. (2003) 'Diagnosis and epidemiology of autism spectrum disorders.' *Canadian Journal of Psychiatry 48*, 517–525.

Tonge, B.J., Brereton, A.V., Gray, K.M. and Einfeld, S.L. (1999) 'Behavioural and emotional disturbance in high-functioning autism and Asperger's disorder.' *Autism: The International Journal of Research and Practice 2*, 117–130.

Venter, A., Lord, C. and Schopler, E. (1992) 'A follow-up study of high-functioning autistic children.' *Journal of Child Psychology and Psychiatry and Allied Disciplines 33*, 3, 489–507.

Volkmar, F., Lord, C., Bailey, A., Schultz, R. and Klin, A. (2004) 'Autism and pervasive developmental disorders.' *Journal of Child Psychology and Psychiatry 45*, 135–170.

Wechsler, D. (1989) *Wechsler Pre-school and Primary Scale of Intelligence – Revised.* San Antonio: The Psychological Corporation.

Wing, L. (1988) 'Autism: possible clues to the underlying pathology. 1: Clinical facts.' In L. Wing (ed) *Aspects of Autism: Biological Research.* Gaskell Psychiatry Series. London: Gaskell.

Wing, L. and Gould, J. (1979) 'Severe impairments of social interaction and associated abnormalities in children: epidemiology and classification.' *Journal of Autism and Developmental Disorders 9*, 11–29.

World Health Organisation (1992) *ICD-10: Classification of Mental and Behavioural Disorders. Clinical Description and Diagnostic Guidelines.* Geneva: World Health Organisation.